100 Ideas for Primary Teachers:

Oracy

Topsy Page

BLOOMSBURY EDUCATION

LONDON OXFORD NEW YORK NEW DELHI SYDNEY

BLOOMSBURY EDUCATION
Bloomsbury Publishing Plc
50 Bedford Square, London, WC1B 3DP, UK
29 Earlsfort Terrace, Dublin 2, Ireland

BLOOMSBURY, BLOOMSBURY EDUCATION and the Diana logo are trademarks of Bloomsbury Publishing Plc

First published in Great Britain, 2024 by Bloomsbury Publishing Plc

This edition published in Great Britain, 2024 by Bloomsbury Publishing Plc

Text copyright © Topsy Page, 2024

Topsy Page has asserted her right under the Copyright, Designs and Patents Act, 1988, to be identified as Author of this work

Bloomsbury Publishing Plc does not have any control over, or responsibility for, any third-party websites referred to or in this book. All internet addresses given in this book were correct at the time of going to press. The author and publisher regret any inconvenience caused if addresses have changed or sites have ceased to exist, but can accept no responsibility for any such changes

The quote used in Idea 9 is from *Fear is the Mind Killer* by Mannion, J. and McAllister, K. reproduced with permission of the Licensor through PLSclear (c) James Mannion and Kate McAllister. The quote used in Idea 50 and some of the talking points in Ideas 53, 74 and 86 are from *Talking Points: Discussion Activities in the Primary Classroom* by Dawes, L. pages 2, 18, 24, 68 and 130 (c) 2012 Lyn Dawes, David Fulton Publishers. Reproduced by permission of Taylor & Francis Group. Reproduced with permission of the Licensor through PLSclear. The quote used in Idea 56 is from *A Dialogic Teaching Companion* by Alexander, R. page 114 reproduced with permission of the Licensor through PLSclear (c) 2020 Robin Alexander. Statements used in Idea 94 are from *Talk Box: Speaking and Listening Activites for Learning at Key Stage 1* by Dawes, L. and Sams, C. page 8 (c) Lyn Dawes and Claire Sams 2004, David Fulton Publishers. Reproduced by permission of Taylor & Francis Group. Reproduced with permission of the Licensor through PLSclear.

Every effort has been made to trace copyright holders and to obtain their permission for the use of copyright material. The publisher apologises for any errors or omissions and would be grateful if notified of any corrections that should be incorporated in future reprints or editions of this book

All rights reserved. No part of this publication may be reproduced or transmitted in any form or by any means, electronic or mechanical, including photocopying, recording, or any information storage or retrieval system, without prior permission in writing from the publishers

A catalogue record for this book is available from the British Library

ISBN: PB: 978-1-8019-9373-9; ePDF: 978-1-8019-9372-2;
ePub: 978-1-8019-9374-6

2 4 6 8 10 9 7 5 3 1 (paperback)

Typeset by Newgen KnowledgeWorks Pvt. Ltd., Chennai, India
Printed and bound in India by Replika Press Pvt. Ltd

To find out more about our authors and books visit www.bloomsbury.com
and sign up for our newsletters

Contents

Acknowledgements	vi
Foreword	vii
Introduction	ix
How to use this book	xi

Part 1: Classroom culture — **1**

1. Three essential ingredients — 2
2. Who's doing most of the talking? — 3
3. How is your teacher talk? — 4
4. Partial thinking welcome! — 5
5. Listen to them! — 6
6. I would like to respectfully challenge — 7
7. *Their* turn to ask the questions — 8
8. The power of peer talk — 9
9. Use oracy to develop metacognition — 10
10. Stop saying fantastic! — 11
11. Hand signals for dialogue — 12
12. RAG cups — 13
13. Thinking Moves A–Z — 14

Part 2: Get everyone talking — **15**

14. Thinking time — 16
15. Daily thinking question — 17
16. Many possible answers — 18
17. Be careful with 'Who can…?' — 19
18. Pupil talk prompts — 20
19. No hands up — 22
20. Random selection — 23
21. Cold calling — 24
22. No more rabbits in headlights! — 25
23. Talking objects — 26
24. Rounds — 27
25. I jot, therefore I talk — 28
26. Everyone together! — 29
27. What about the 'quiet children'? — 30
28. Please could you speak a bit louder? — 32
29. The volumiser — 33
30. Cut-ups — 34

31	Contribution counters	35
32	Jigsaw	36
33	Tailored talk prompts	37
34	Oracy to develop reflective learners	38

Part 3: Learning to listen — **39**
35	Don't expect it to just happen!	40
36	Reduce repetition	42
37	What does bad listening look like?	43
38	Look at the speaker	44
39	Check your class	45
40	What do you think about what Janie said?	46
41	Talk towers	47
42	How do we know they are listening?	48

Part 4: Talking in pairs — **49**
43	What makes a good talk partner?	50
44	Set them up for success	51
45	Who's first?	52
46	Changing partners	53
47	Talk prompts for talk partners	54
48	Make sure they're on task!	55

Part 5: Talking in small groups — **57**
49	Ground rules	58
50	Exploratory talk	59
51	Bad discussion/good discussion?	60
52	Discussion roles	61
53	Talking points	62
54	Placemat consensus	64

Part 6: Whole-class talk — **65**
55	Dialogue	66
56	Teacher talk moves	68
57	P4C	70
58	Tell *us*	71
59	Circles are worth it!	72
60	Speaker chooses	73
61	Popcorn	74
62	Stand up to speak up	75
63	They ramble on!	76

Part 7: Talk for different purposes — **77**
64	The art of argument	78
65	Common ground	79
66	Public speaking takes practice!	80

67	Tell us a story!	82
68	Talking to build friendships	83
69	Experimenting with ways of speaking	84

Part 8: Talk games — 85

70	Find someone who…	86
71	Would you rather?	87
72	Good idea/bad idea?	88
73	Odd one out	89
74	Four corners	90
75	What would you do if…?	91
76	The beanbag game	92
77	The imagination game	93
78	Word connect	94
79	Ten-word challenge	95
80	Give one, get one	96
81	Yes, and…	97
82	Opinion continuums	98
83	Bring it to life!	99
84	PMIQ	100
85	Don't forget barrier games!	101

Part 9: Embedding oracy — 103

86	Infuse your curriculum with oracy	104
87	Oracy Skills Framework	106
88	Practising the four strands	107
89	Vision for talk	108
90	Talk promise	109
91	Talking Tuesdays	110
92	Let's talk about talk	111
93	Oracy lesson structure	112
94	Are they getting better at talking?	113
95	Use talk to develop vocabulary	114
96	Talk-based outcomes	116
97	Oracy opportunities	117
98	Parental engagement	118
99	What do your pupils think about oracy?	119
100	Leading oracy	120

References and further reading — 123

Acknowledgements

Thanks to the following people for their support and dialogue during the creation of this book: Monica Baart, Vanessa Dewey, Natasha Dunne, Jonathan Evans, Frances Gregory, Halima Hakim, Kate Holmes, Mel Klein, James Mannion, Krista Maxwell, Ruth Nutton-Jones, Dilys Page, Laura Patchett, Neil Phillipson, Luke Roberts, Claire Shercliffe, David Trent, Rosie Wilson and Jane Yates.

Special thanks to the following colleagues, whose work influenced or directly contributed to specific ideas: Edward de Bono for PMI; Lyn Dawes for Talking points and Don't expect it to just happen; Alan Howe for Tell us a story; Sarah Jane Henderson for Partial thinking; Neil Mercer for Exploratory talk, Ground rules and Bad discussion/good discussion; Cathy O'Connor and Sarah Michaels for Teacher talk moves; Will Ord for Talk towers; Helen Parry for the Volumiser; Sara Stanley for Daily thinking question and Good idea/bad idea; Roger Sutcliffe for the Thinking Moves A–Z, Ten-word challenge, the Q of PMIQ and Last three to speak; Dylan Wiliam for RAG cups and Random selection; and Steve Williams for QI books.

Particular thanks to Sarah Jane Henderson and Alan Howe for ongoing inspiration and conversations about pedagogy.

And above all, thanks to Dan.

Foreword

This book by our Oracy Cambridge colleague Topsy is informed by significant and reliable research on talk in classrooms. As in her workshops, she has translated the essential messages of that research into clear, useful and practical ideas for teachers. These ideas do not come from ivory towers or laboratory experiments. Rather, our work has typically involved going out into schools to find out what the best teachers do that makes them so effective in helping their students to learn, then trying to distil the essence of what we find into information which will help all teachers develop their own practice. And the ideas in this book were not only generated by work at Cambridge, but also by other researchers and teachers worldwide.

Oracy is a term invented by Professor Andrew Wilkinson back in the 1960s, as part of an attempt to give spoken language a similar status in educational policy and practice to that traditionally given to written language. It simply means the capability to get things done effectively through speaking and listening. It applies not only to the development of children's spoken language skills but also to teachers' effective use and management of talk in the classroom to enable their pupils to learn. In this book, you will find a wide range of practical ideas to make oracy come alive in educational settings.

It has taken some decades, but at the time of writing it seems that oracy is starting to be given the attention it deserves. I think Topsy would agree with me that we rarely need to convince primary teachers of its importance; but there is also, at the time of writing, a groundswell of political interest which may at last give oracy its proper place in educational policy as well as practice. While this book is intended for a teacher audience (who I am sure will find it extremely useful), I think policy makers – and parents – could also learn much from what is here.

Professor Neil Mercer

Oracy Cambridge: the Hughes Hall Centre for Effective Spoken Communication, University of Cambridge

Introduction

Imagine a classroom where every child speaks confidently. Where every child can be clearly heard sharing their individual thoughts and ideas. A classroom where children work productively in pairs and groups, where children support and challenge each other, listening with respect and encouragement.

Imagine a classroom where everyone knows that *talking can help us think* and *thinking can help us talk*. Where children express themselves clearly, are interested in each other's thoughts and ask each other questions because they know it helps them learn.

Imagine a world where our pupils grow up wanting to understand different perspectives, knowing how to disagree respectfully and feeling confident to stand up for themselves and others.

Oracy makes all this possible. It gives children a chance to develop a voice and be able to use that voice effectively in relationships, in work, in life. If children can't do these things, they won't thrive. Oracy is a matter of social justice, citizenship and democracy.

Oracy in the primary classroom means:

1. managing classroom talk to deepen learning across the curriculum
2. equipping your pupils to use spoken language effectively in any situation.

This book provides the tools to help you do these two things.

Five things to keep in mind:

- **Don't label children as 'quiet' or 'shy'**. A label can become a self-fulfilling prophecy. Children are developing all the time and it's our job to help them develop. They may not be speaking much *at the moment* simply because they haven't had the opportunity to find their voice.

- **Value all accents and dialects** – they are an important part of children's identities.

- Many of the activities in this book include structures and scaffolds, making them accessible and beneficial for **multilingual learners** and **children with additional needs**.

- **Know why you're doing it**. Familiarise yourself with the underlying purpose of each idea, so you can choose the right approach for the right moment and use it skilfully.
- **Stick at it**. While some strategies can have immediate results, others take longer to bear fruit, because they are about a change in culture. Remember that new habits take time to embed.

I'd love to hear any stories about your oracy journey. Contact me via www.topsypage.com.

How to use this book

This book includes simple, practical, tried-and-tested ideas to enable you to develop and promote oracy in your class and school.

Each idea includes:

- a catchy title, easy to refer to and share with your colleagues
- an interesting quote linked to the idea
- a summary of the idea in bold, making it easy to flick through the book and identify an idea you want to use at a glance
- a step-by-step guide to implementing the idea.

Each idea also includes one or more of the following:

Teaching tip	Taking it further	Bonus idea ★
Practical tips and advice for how and how not to run the activity or put the idea into practice.	Ideas and advice for how to extend the idea or develop it further.	**There are 57 bonus ideas in this book that are extra-exciting, extra-original and extra-interesting.**

Share how you use these ideas and find out what other practitioners have done using **#100ideas**.

Classroom culture

Part 1

IDEA 1

Three essential ingredients

They know that I expect them to talk, that I expect them to give explanations and reasons. *Year 2 teacher*

For oracy to flourish, it's vital to have the right classroom culture.

> **Teaching tip**
>
> Praise pupils for listening well and valuing others' thoughts: 'Thank you for your respectful listening, Jonny – you really thought about what Clara said.'

1. Have high expectations...
All your pupils can get better at communicating. *Do not underestimate them.* Pupils respond to our expectations:

- 'When you respond, I expect you to give detail.'
- 'Please elaborate, Jack.'
- 'Say it again, Simran, using our focus vocabulary.'
- 'I'm going to be calling on you to find out what you think.'

Use a kind, respectful tone at all times. (This is not about mocking or intimidating pupils.)

If a child doesn't immediately respond during whole-class talk, stay with them, support them and find out what they are thinking.

2. ...while being caring and thoughtful
All children have different starting points, and some are initially less confident with their oracy skills. *Without losing your high expectations, be sensitive and nurturing.* This can be a delicate balance; the key is to challenge at the appropriate level.

3. Create a culture of listening
For children to talk confidently, and to risk sharing thoughts, emotions or new ideas, they need to feel safe. They need to know they will be listened to with respect – by everyone. *They need to know everyone will value their contribution.* Ground rules will help with this (Ideas 49 and 90). See also Idea 5 and Part 3.

> **Bonus idea** ★
>
> Make your classroom accessible to all learners by using pictorial or 'PECS' symbols. Search online for 'communication-friendly checklists' for further ideas.

IDEA 2

Who's doing most of the talking?

They talk too much! Usually they take ages to send us to our seats to start working. I'm always thinking, can they be shorter and quicker?
Age 8

There isn't one correct classroom talk ratio. Effective teacher talk plays a critical role – for example, modelling, explaining and questioning. The amount needed will vary from lesson to lesson. However, sometimes teacher talk is excessive and doesn't impact on learning.

Have a look at this conversation:
Teacher: Why do you think you weren't allowed through the gate? Do you think fire is dangerous?
Pupil: Yes.
Teacher: Did you see lots of fireworks? Were there lots of nice colours? What colours were they?
Pupil: Golden.
Teacher: There were some golden? Super!

Imagine if the teacher had paused after their first question, or encouraged the child to elaborate.

Think about *your* lessons
- Who is talking most – you or your pupils?
- Is your talk impacting on learning?
- When your pupils respond, how many words do they usually use?
- Do you encourage them to expand?
- Do you value their thoughts and opinions?

Ways to change the ratio
1 Plan talk tasks (see Idea 86).
2 Ask pupils to read out learning objectives or instructions, instead of you.
3 Have pupils speak instead of you. For example, explaining a method or concept, spelling a word or opening an assembly.
4 Use your teacher talk to develop dialogue (see Idea 56).

> **Teaching tip**
>
> Bite your lip! After a pupil speaks, pause. Don't immediately jump in. With practice, this will become a positive new habit.

> **Taking it further**
>
> Pupils tune out when we repeat instructions multiple times. Use concise written and pictorial instructions sometimes, instead of verbal.

> **Bonus idea** ★
>
> **Instead of using your voice, try sound signals. For example, train your pupils that when they hear the 30-second *Countdown* theme tune, it means 'Stop what you are doing and come to the carpet before the music finishes!'**

IDEA 3

How is your teacher talk?

We must select what we say with the same awareness and deliberateness as we would when we select and use other resources.
Joan Tough

Be a good role-model for oracy. Listen to your own teacher talk and plan key parts of it.

We all know that modelling is a powerful tool for teaching. That means that all of your talk is influencing your pupils. Don't leave it to chance – improvised questions and explanations are often low-quality and can result in us repeating and rephrasing many times.

Try to develop the habit of hearing yourself talk while you teach. This is part of being a reflective teacher and will help you slow down, give thinking time, ask better questions and ensure that your teacher talk is having impact on learning.

Plan your questions
Decide that a critical part of lesson planning will be taking time to plan key questions to get everyone thinking and talking.

Practise your explanations
Listen to your explanations when you teach. How effective are they? Try practising them. Start by focusing on core concepts or key words and decide exactly how you will explain them.

Fine-tune your instructions
Listen to your instructions – are they clear and concise? Do you repeat? Do you sometimes ask questions instead of giving clear instructions? Instead of asking 'Shall we read our story now?' be clear: 'Story time! Come to the carpet.'

> **Taking it further**
>
> Do a question audit. Ask an additional adult to note down all the questions you ask. Analyse them afterwards and reflect: which ones had impact on learning?

> **Bonus idea** ★
>
> Audio-record yourself teach and play it back to hear the impact of your talk.

IDEA 4

Partial thinking welcome!

It creates an incredibly safe space to share ideas. *Headteacher*

Expressing thoughts that aren't completely formed can be useful both to the speaker and to others. Some schools call this 'partial thinking' and they model, encourage and value it.

Partial thinking creates an atmosphere of collaboration and learning together: pupils gain confidence to articulate emerging ideas.

In a classroom where partial thinking is part of the culture, you will hear phrases like these:
- I'm not certain, but...
- I wonder if...
- I'm not completely sure, but what I'm thinking is...
- One reason could be...
- That's making me think...
- I'm now wondering whether...

Thoughts don't always come to us fully formed. If we expect children to always give complete, fully reasoned responses or thoughts, we'll miss out on a lot of valuable thinking.

How to do it

Let pupils know you're interested in what they're thinking and that all ideas can lead to learning. Use phrases that encourage pupils to express their thinking:

- Could you tell us a bit of what you're thinking, Annie?
- What's in your head, Yusuf? Even if you don't have a complete answer, we still want to know what you're thinking.
- Which bit are you finding tricky?

It's essential to use an encouraging tone and positive body language, and that pupils listen respectfully to each other (see Part 3).

Teaching tip

Welcoming partial thinking isn't about accepting random ideas or incoherent thoughts! When necessary, prompt pupils to explain their thinking and back up their ideas.

Taking it further

Partial thinking and exploratory talk (Idea 50) are types of 'thinking talk'. There is a difference between these and more formal 'presentational talk' (see Idea 66). It's important that pupils have opportunities to learn the skills of both.

IDEA 5

Listen to them!

Mum, you're not listening properly to me! You're being just like the teachers! They never let me finish what I'm saying! *Age 11*

Children are more likely to talk if they know we're genuinely listening. But classrooms are busy places, and listening carefully requires a lot of effort. Often we have ideas in our head, including what we hope pupils will say. This makes it hard to listen.

Sometimes when we should be listening to a pupil, we're doing something else. What are your habits? When you're supposed to be listening, are you ever thinking about something that happened earlier, or what you're planning to do next? Are you thinking about what you hope the child will say, or making an assumption about the quality of their response? Instead of listening, are you getting ready to stop or interrupt them?

Taking it further

During whole-class talk, take notes. Scribe key words on the board. These are proof of listening, and habits your pupils may pick up (see Idea 25).

What to do

1 When a pupil is speaking, *wait for them to finish*. Then wait a few more seconds. This pause gives you time to process what they said. It also gives them the chance to say more.
2 *Be open* to hearing what they're saying. Try not to always have an answer in your head.
3 Respond in a way that makes it clear you're interested and *listening to understand*. Teacher talk moves (Idea 56) will help with this.
4 If you realise you haven't completely heard what a pupil said, ask them to repeat. 'Julia, I'm sorry, please could you repeat your point?'
5 *Check you've definitely understood* what they said. 'Let me check, are you saying…?'
6 *Reflect on your own biases and assumptions* – this is hard work, but the first step is to be aware. Labelling children is damaging and will stop you having high expectations.

Bonus idea ★

Take time to practise genuinely listening for a few moments here and there in your own life!

IDEA 6

I would like to respectfully challenge

They can avoid conflicts now — fewer arguments about who is right or who is wrong. They listen to each other more. It's made them a lot calmer. *Year 5 ECT*

Create a classroom culture where challenge is welcome, and is regarded as a key part of learning.

It's a great sign when pupils express disagreement, because it shows they're thinking! Provide prompts that permit and encourage them to politely challenge:
- 'I have a different idea…'
- 'Excuse me, Jade, but I think I disagree…'
- 'I would like to respectfully challenge.'
- 'I would like to politely disagree.'

Play games such as good idea/bad idea (Idea 72) to practise using these prompts.

Display the prompts so they are accessible in every lesson.

Praise: 'I love the way you're challenging so politely, Sami.'

Model polite challenge over and over again. For example, 'Excuse me, Mr H, I think you've made a mistake with your spelling.'

The benefits are many:
- Your pupils learn how to disagree politely — a hugely important life skill.
- Your pupils look out for misconceptions among their peers and start to address them through dialogue. Suddenly you're not the only one checking for understanding!
- Thinking becomes deeper — pupils are motivated to think about what others say.
- Teaching and learning become more enjoyable; everyone is more engaged.

Teaching tip

Initially, many children are surprised when you invite and encourage disagreement. Emphasise that it's useful to challenge each other, as long as it's done politely.

Taking it further

Work towards creating a genuine culture of respectful dialogue among your colleagues, including high-quality listening and constructive criticism. Children will see and hear that this is normal and useful. They will absorb this way of being.

IDEA 7

Their turn to ask the questions

Sometimes I've got some questions, but we have to move on. *Age 8*

In schools, most questions related to learning come from teachers — pupils need to ask questions too!

Asking questions is a core oracy skill for life and learning. Get your pupils skilled at asking questions to find out more, to clarify and to develop their thinking and curiosity. Once this habit is developed, questions can permeate everything and become part of your classroom ethos. Questions are also a useful window into pupil interests, prior knowledge, understanding, confusion and misconceptions.

Question time

At key moments, ask pupils, 'What questions do you have?' Set an expectation that everyone thinks of a question related to the learning. Make sure you leave time to hear the questions; if your class think you're rushing, they won't ask. You want pupils to realise that questions have an important role in learning.

For example, at the start of a lesson, as part of activating prior knowledge, invite pupils to work in pairs or trios to generate questions, as well as discuss what they already know: 'With your partner, jot five facts, and five questions, about the Tudors.' Use their questions to inform your teaching.

Pupil questions provide a good opportunity for dialogue. Encourage others in the room to answer them, inviting further pupils to build or challenge as necessary. Of course, use your teacher talk to answer complex questions, or address misconceptions, when necessary.

> **Teaching tip**
>
> The phrase 'Some questions.' followed by an expectant pause usually generates more questions than 'Any questions?'!

> **Taking it further**
>
> Check out QFT from the Right Question Institute — search online for 'Question Formulation Technique'. Or read their inspiring and practical book *Make Just One Change* (Rothstein and Santana, 2011).

> **Bonus idea** ★
>
> Give every pupil a card with a question mark on it. Encourage them to show this whenever they have a question about the learning. This will immediately raise the status of pupil questions.

IDEA 8

The power of peer talk

I'll help you! Here, let's look at our sound mat. Age 5

You're not the only one who can transmit knowledge, explain, question and clarify. Your pupils can too!

Work to create an informal, positive, ongoing culture of peer support

1. Tell pupils you want them to support each other with their learning – give them permission to work collaboratively.
2. Tell them to use quiet voices.
3. Listen for children supporting each other, and celebrate this.

Most peer support will be small things such as asking partners, 'Do you know how to spell "fire"?' But this can have a huge impact. Children aren't sitting waiting for the teacher. They become proactive, independent problem solvers.

Provide structured peer critique opportunities

- Have pupils compare answers in pairs or trios. If answers vary, pupils support each other to figure out where someone has gone wrong and help them understand how to fix it.
- Show children's work to the class (use a visualiser). Say, 'Talk to your partner about what you see. What impresses you? What specific suggestions for improvement could you make?'

Useful phrases for peer critique

I really like…	One thing you could think about is…
Something I'm impressed by is…	I've spotted a mistake in paragraph two…
Something you've done well is…	One way you could make this better is…
It's effective how…	Can you find a way to…?
It's great that you…	I am wondering if…?

Taking it further

Search online for 'Austin's butterfly video' and 'Shirley Clarke literacy instructions video' for two brilliant examples of peer critique.

Bonus idea ★

Use 'pause points' for moments of paired peer discussion during a written task. In pairs, children read each other's work and suggest improvements. Each child then makes their own changes. Give each pause point a separate focus such as punctuation or vocabulary. Peer critique while working on a task means improvements are made in the moment.

IDEA 9

Use oracy to develop metacognition

To develop metacognition in our students, we must first teach them to articulate their thoughts. *James Mannion, Rethinking Education*

Language is the route into being aware of thinking, and learning to manage it better. Pupils who are metacognitive — can reflect on, verbalise and manage their own thinking — are more effective learners. They are aware of their own thinking approaches. They continually reflect on how their learning is going, and adjust strategies when needed.

Here are four ways to use classroom talk to develop pupils' metacognitive skills.

1. Get them thinking together
Learning how to think together (Idea 50) helps children to manage their own thinking. They try out different thinking strategies and hear classmates doing the same. Gradually they build a wider repertoire of thinking strategies to call on during independent learning.

2. Model thinking
The more you make your own thinking 'visible', the more your pupils will develop awareness of their thinking. For example, model thinking aloud in maths: 'I wonder if cubes might help me with this problem. Or maybe a different piece of equipment. The numbers are quite big. Hmm... perhaps a number line will help.'

3. Encourage pupils to think aloud
Ask pupils to discuss how they might tackle a task and what strategies might help them. Sometimes, pause them mid-way through to reflect out loud in pairs and change their strategies if necessary. At the end, have them reflect again.

4. Provide a vocabulary for thinking
Thinking Moves A–Z (Idea 13) gives everyone a common language to discuss ways of thinking.

> **Taking it further**
>
> Search online for the EEF Questioning Habits Tool on their Metacognition and Self-Regulated Learning page.

> **Bonus idea** ★
>
> Listen out for and positively comment on different types of thinking: 'It was useful that you made a connection there, Jacquie.', 'I noticed you really testing out that assumption, Tayshan – that helped us think more deeply.'

IDEA 10

Stop saying fantastic!

If you give really specific comments about something impressive, it inspires others to up their game. *Headteacher*

Positivity alone isn't enough. Use your teacher talk to give specific praise — identifying exactly what you think is good or fantastic. This has greater impact because the child knows *what* they did well. Specific praise empowers children to reflect, to improve their learning or behaviour, and to become confident, independent learners.

Instead of saying...	Try saying...
Good girl, Lizzy!	Great talking, Lizzy!
Super!	Super listening!
Good boy	I really like all the maths language you used.
Well done	I heard you reading your work aloud to check it — well done.
Lovely	Lovely straight underlining, Jamal.
Good work, Ria	You remembered your full stop, Ria – good work.
That's great!	That's careful counting, Mark! I love the way you touch each object.
Fantastic, Katya!	I really like the way you justified your opinion, Katya.
Great!	What a lovely clear voice! We could all hear that!
Amazing!	Amazing perseverance, Antoni, you kept trying different strategies.

Make sure your praise is honest. Only praise things that you are genuinely pleased with.

Teaching tip

Keep your teacher talk positive. Use it to develop positive behaviour by giving specific praise to pupils who are on task. Avoid public reprimands or negative comments to children. If you need to mention poor behaviour choices, do it one-to-one and use a quiet voice.

Taking it further

Read more on praise: search for 'Carol Dweck The Perils and Promises of Praise'.

Bonus idea ★

To gain the habit of specific praise, choose one or two talk stems that you will use frequently. For example: 'Thank you for...', 'I love the way you are...'

IDEA 11

Hand signals for dialogue

Hand signals mean we all have to show what we think and not all shout out. *Age 10*

Use active learning signals to indicate 'I agree', 'I disagree' or 'I'd like to build on…'

Decide on a set of non-verbal signals to indicate thinking during whole-class dialogue. Aim for still, silent signals, which are less likely to be distracting than moving or noisy ones.

For example:
- Open hand resting on heart – I agree.
- Closed hand on heart – I disagree.
- Thumbs and index fingers make two interlocking circles – I have something to say that connects.
- Index finger up – I have a question.

Give opportunities to practise.

Benefits
- Pupils have a mechanism to challenge each other. This changes everything! They now have permission to query what is being said, spot misconceptions, respectfully disagree and so on.
- Class dialogue goes deeper – pupils can ask peers why they disagree with them or look for peers who can support their point.
- Thinking becomes visible. You, or pupils, can ask others, 'Why do you disagree?'
- Hand signals help pupils to self-regulate. If they can show their thinking, they are less likely to shout out.
- Everyone can see when others are listening.
- Even if there isn't time for everyone to speak, everyone can indicate an opinion.

> **Teaching tip**
>
> Warning! It's essential that your class use hand signals respectfully, and that this fits with your class ethos of respectful listening and positive attitude to learning. Discuss how the timing of hand signals matters. There are pros and cons of showing signals while people are talking. Discuss the possible effects of 'jumping in' with a disagreement signal when someone is still making their justification.

IDEA 12

RAG cups

They're really very good because you can say if you're not confident by changing your cup. *Age 9*

A powerful tool for assessment for learning, and talk.

RAG cups are red, amber and green paper cups which some schools make available to every child in every lesson. The expectation is that children will continuously reflect on their learning, asking themselves 'How is my learning going?' throughout the lesson, and showing their answer using the cups.

Red = 'I'm stuck' or 'I disagree'
Amber = 'I'm a bit confused' or 'I have a question'
Green = 'I understand', 'I can teach others' or 'I agree'

Give a set of cups to each child. The cups stay on tables at all times. Tell the class to start each lesson by stacking their cups with green showing. As the lesson progresses, they are responsible for changing the colour to reflect their learning status.

- During whole-class learning, if you spot a child on amber or red, pause. Use pupil talk to progress – for example, ask another child, whose cup is showing green, to explain. (The cups develop accountability as well as oracy – children on green are expected to be able to give peer support.) If you see a lot of amber or red, consider alternative strategies, including different ways to explain.
- When pupils are working on their own, if peers notice someone on red, they can support: 'Are you OK, Emeka? Do you need help?'
- When pupils are working on their own, adults can see where to support: 'I see you're feeling unsure, Amy – why are you on amber?'

> **Teaching tip**
>
> Invest time in this to reap the rewards. Be consistent with your expectations. This is about children gaining the habit of reflecting on their learning continuously.

> **Taking it further**
>
> RAG cups are brilliant when pupils present work to the class. Classmates can change their cups if they spot any errors and then explain and make suggestions for improvements.

> **Bonus idea** ★
>
> During whole-class or group dialogue, children use their cups to signal agree/disagree.

IDEA 13

Thinking Moves A–Z

We have seen tremendous growth in our students' ability to explain and evaluate their own thinking. *Year 2 teacher*

Thinking Moves A–Z, developed by Roger Sutcliffe, gives us a way to use metacognition every day in the classroom. By covering all types of thinking in a memorable list, it provides a language for teachers and pupils to talk about and reflect on their own cognitive processes — enhancing thinking and deepening learning.

Taking it further

Every move has an icon and a hand sign. Check out the book *Thinking Moves A–Z: Metacognition Made Simple* (Roger Sutcliffe et al., 2019) and training from DialogueWorks.

Thinking Move	Possible talk prompt
AHEAD	I predict that …
BACK	It was mentioned earlier that…
CONNECT	Connecting to what Toni said…
DIVIDE	I think that is different because…
EXPLAIN	I think that Craig means…
FORMULATE	I'd like to add a new point…
GROUP	What these have in common is…
HEADLINE	The most important point is…
INFER	There's evidence to suggest…
JUSTIFY	I'm certain of this because…
KEYWORD	The big ideas are…
LOOK/LISTEN	I'm noticing that…
MAINTAIN	Personally, I think…
NEGATE	I would like to challenge…
ORDER	A good method might be…
PICTURE	If I were…
QUESTION	What if…?
RESPOND	Alina's point made me think…
SIZE	Statistics show…
TEST	I doubt that…
USE	The purpose of this is…
VARY	Another way of looking at it…
WEIGH UP	I can see both sides, but…
eXEMPLIFY	I'd like to give an example…
YIELD	I've changed my thinking…
ZOOM in	Let's focus in on the idea that…
ZOOM out	It's important to consider the bigger picture…

Get everyone talking

Part 2

IDEA 14

Thinking time

I won't have an answer if there's no thinking time. *Age 8*

Thinking time dramatically improves the quality of spoken responses and gets more pupils involved.

Teaching tip
Use a symbol on your slides to remind you and your class that thinking time is needed.

Taking it further
Check out the fascinating paper 'Using "think-time" and "wait-time" skillfully in the classroom' (Robert Stahl, 1994), about eight moments where silence is useful in learning.

Bonus idea ★
Use a thinking action such as hand on chin. Or say, 'Show me your thinking faces!'

Ways to create a culture of thinking time
- Remind pupils: 'Thinking is an essential part of learning.'
- Embrace silence as useful rather than awkward. Don't rush to fill every silence with teacher talk!
- When you ask questions, pause or say, 'I'll give you some thinking time.'
- Give a visual signal to indicate 'stop and think'. For example, palm up like stopping traffic.
- Model that teachers also need time to think: 'Hmm, let me think about that.'
- When something interesting or tricky comes up, say, 'Let's all have a think about that.'
- Give specific praise for thinking: 'I can see you're really thinking about that, Jake.'
- Empower pupils to request thinking time (see Idea 22).
- Encourage jotting during thinking time.
- Set high expectations: 'I'll expect you to contribute after you've had a think.'

Adjust the amount of thinking time depending on question type, pupil age, type of response required, prior learning and how recently they last encountered the content. Provide three seconds minimum.

Silent thinking time is useful for everyone in the class. 'Eager talkers' become more articulate; 'quieter ones' become more confident to speak because they have their thoughts in order. Similarly, thinking time is a great enabler for many pupils with additional needs.

IDEA 15

Daily thinking question

The children really enjoy it! Some of them have now started to ask me 'What do you think, Miss?' and 'Why do you think that?'
Headteacher

A fun thinking question every day engages pupils to talk and share their opinions.

Developed by Sara Stanley, this is a wonderful way to give children a voice and get them to express themselves. It also helps them to realise that it's OK to have different opinions to others. Pupils quickly become more confident to talk and improve their reasoning skills.

Provide a thought-provoking question to pupils every day. Give them some time to talk about it with peers or adults. Make this part of the daily routine – first thing in the morning, in the dinner hall or straight after lunch.

Make sure each question allows for, and encourages, different opinions. This avoids the fear of 'getting the wrong answer'. Set an expectation that pupils explain their reasons.

Questions that require children to make a choice are particularly effective, especially with younger children or children who are less confident to talk:

- Would you rather look after a giant puppy or a tiny rhino?
- Would you rather get information from friends or from the internet?
- Presents every day – good idea/bad idea?
- Ban plastic packaging – good idea/bad idea?

See also Ideas 71 and 72.

Once your class have gained confidence, you can also ask big, open questions like 'Can money buy happiness?' or 'What if everyone made up their own rules?'

Teaching tip

When you first introduce the daily thinking question, model making a choice and giving a reason until your pupils get used to it. You may also need to prompt them for reasons. Eventually, pupils will offer their reasons without you asking them.

Taking it further

Send the daily thinking question home via your school app, website or newsletter.

Bonus idea ★

Give pupils a way of physically indicating their choice – for example, cubes or lolly sticks with names on. This promotes engagement and accountability. Search online for 'Topsy Page daily question video' for more information.

IDEA 16

Many possible answers

I couldn't believe it – children who never talk, talked! *Year 4 teacher*

Take away the fear of talking by asking questions that do not have one single correct answer.

Think back over your last day of teaching. How many questions did you ask? What type of questions were they? How many had a single correct answer? How many were open questions?

If most learning in your classroom revolves around closed questions – questions that have one correct answer – this will limit which pupils want to speak.

If you deliberately include more thinking and opinion questions, more children will offer their thoughts. Your pupils will realise that all responses are valued, as long as they're accompanied by thoughtful reasons.

Questions with many possible answers also encourage children to be independent thinkers, and develop both creative and critical thinking.

Start planning 'many possible answers' questions across the curriculum. Use question structures to help you:

- **Would you rather** be a child in a Stone Age village or a child here and now? (See Idea 71.)
- Climbing volcanoes – **good idea/bad idea?** (See Idea 72.)
- Which is the **odd one out** – piano, tambourine or recorder? (See Idea 73.)
- **Four corners:** The internet has a negative effect on human communication. Strongly agree? Agree? Strongly disagree? Disagree? (See Idea 74.)

Be transparent with the class: tell them that there isn't just one right answer.

Teaching tip

Questions with many possible answers make great talk starter tasks. For example, if you are beginning some work on famous explorers, ask your class: Being an explorer – good idea/bad idea? You could also ask this again at the end of the learning, to find out whether anyone's thinking has changed.

Bonus idea ★

There are lots of other ways to create questions with many possible answers across the curriculum. Search online for 'question matrix' or 'low floor high ceiling'. See also Idea 57.

IDEA 17

Be careful with 'Who can...?'

I didn't realise how much I said 'Who can...?' I now see that it was always the same children volunteering to speak. Now I use strategies to make sure every voice is heard. *Year 1 ECT*

Starting questions with 'Who can...?' allows children to opt out of learning. Use alternative phrasing to bring everyone into the conversation.

How we ask questions greatly affects how many children think and talk in lessons.

Think about your teacher questions. Do you phrase things in ways that encourage only the more confident pupils to volunteer? If you do, it's likely that the same children will respond time after time. This won't enable others to become confident talkers.

Teaching tip

Remember that giving pupils time for oral rehearsal with a partner can greatly improve fluency, clarity and confidence to speak.

Instead of	Try
Who'd like to read out paragraph 1?	Suki, read paragraph 1 please.
Who can remember what we did yesterday in geography?	Discuss in pairs three things we learned yesterday about the Amazon.
Who can tell me what 'adverb' means?	Look back at yesterday's work. [PAUSE] Bea, tell us about adverbs.
Is there anyone who would like to share?	When you've finished jotting, I'll pick a stick. (See Ideas 25 and 20.)

For children who lack confidence, provide frequent opportunities to talk to the class – choose them purposefully. This will enable them to become more confident. See also Idea 19.

IDEA 18

Pupil talk prompts

The talk prompts are a real winner, with a noticeable knock-on effect on self-esteem in the classroom. *Deputy head*

Pupil talk prompts are sentence starters that instantly improve confidence and the quality of talk.

Providing your pupils with talk prompts can change the quality of talk almost immediately. Prompts give confidence to join in, enable more powerful, articulate speech, expand vocabulary, and impact on writing.

Introduce them to your class and before long your pupils will be building on each others' points and respectfully disagreeing. Talk prompts are inclusive; they can help all children to start off a spoken sentence with confidence. Even children who are new to English will find prompts they can use. This can be an empowering experience.

Suggested prompts
- I think... I strongly believe... It is my opinion that... (stating an idea)
- Please could you clarify that? Please could you explain what you mean? (clarifying or checking)
- What if... Some people think... (seeing things from a different perspective)
- I agree... I agree with Sara because... (supporting or agreeing)
- I have a different idea... I disagree... I would like to challenge something that Samia said... I would like to respectfully challenge... (challenging or disagreeing)
- Adding to what Isaac said... Building on what Ella said... I have been listening carefully and I would like to add a new point... (expanding or building on)

Teaching tip
You can find a free printable pdf talk prompts resource at topsypage.com

Taking it further
At first, as pupils try out talk prompts, they may sound clunky and they may choose the wrong prompt sometimes. As they gain expertise, don't let the prompts become limiting or restrictive. Once your class are confident with them, and using them effectively, encourage them to vary the wording or make up some new ones. For example, 'I would like to respectfully disagree' or 'Personally I would prefer to...' Ultimately the prompts should become redundant!

- I think Mo is saying that... In other words, Matt is saying... (paraphrasing or rewording)
- Why is it that...? I am wondering if... I'm not certain but... I'm not completely sure but what I'm thinking is... (thinking aloud or sharing partial thinking)
- If _____ then... I know _____ because... (justifying or giving reasons)
- Elis, what do you think? Ben, what do you think about what I said? Carys, do you agree or disagree? (passing on the dialogue)

Embedding pupil talk prompts

- **Display the prompts** on classroom walls or write a couple of them on your whiteboard next to the date. You could introduce a few at a time – for example, start with and 'I agree' and 'I disagree'.
- For older children, provide **a sheet of all the prompts** on tables so they have access to them all the time.
- As with all language that you want your pupils to use, the more you **model it**, the more they will use it, and the more they will use it correctly. For example, 'Building on what Nadia said, if we use a metaphor here, it could add interest.'

Here are some other ways to remind your pupils of the talk prompts:

- When children are talking in a circle, place large prompts in the centre.
- When children are talking in small groups, place prompts on their tables.
- Keep an additional set of prompts available for interventions, to ensure that all children have consistent access to them.

> **Teaching tip**
>
> Provide specific opportunities every week to practise using the prompts. See Ideas 15, 73 and 91.

> **Bonus idea** ★
>
> Colour-code the prompts according to category.

IDEA 19

No hands up

When it's hands up they pick the smart children... *Age 10*

Stop using only your reliable speakers! Hands up usually only involves a fraction of the class. There are other ways to find out what your pupils are thinking — soon you will have everybody involved in the learning.

Using hands up to decide who speaks is common. Unfortunately, it often means that the same few pupils talk. This creates a risk that teachers rely on these same confident speakers. Hands up also sends messages that it's optional to participate in learning, and, to those who are feeling less confident, that their ideas are not valuable.

Try asking your pupils what they think about hands up. Here's what some children have said:
- 'My hand is always tired!'
- 'Hands up isn't fair because some people sit back and let others do the work.'
- 'Sometimes more thinking time is needed.'

Pupils who are less confident at speaking will not become more confident unless they are given opportunities. Reduce your reliance on hands up, and try other ways of managing who speaks:
- Random selection (Idea 20)
- Cold calling (Idea 21)
- Speaker chooses (Idea 60)
- Rounds (Idea 24)
- Popcorn (Idea 61).

Another option is random groupings. Pupils take a coloured cube as they enter the classroom. When it's time for talk, pick a colour: 'Green cubes — your turn to share your ideas.'

> **Teaching tip**
>
> Don't allow children to raise hands but then ask a child who doesn't have their hand up. This causes confusion and frustration — especially for pupils waiting with their hands up. Be transparent! Tell them: 'No hands up now. I'm going to be calling on different people to find out what you're thinking.' (Idea 21) Or: 'Popcorn now — share what you did.' (Idea 61) Or: 'Over to you — speaker chooses.' (Idea 60) This way, everyone knows what they are supposed to be doing.

IDEA 20

Random selection

It's made some of the shy people much more confident to talk. *Age 11*

Have a set of lolly sticks – one with each child's name. Ask a question, give thinking time and then pull out a stick.

Random selection approaches immediately increase pupil participation. Suddenly, it's not just the same few children talking. Everyone realises their stick might be selected, so they need to have something to say. Children also appreciate the fairness of random selection. It removes teacher bias, conscious or unconscious.

Warning! Don't let this useful tool generate anxiety, nor be wasted. As with cold calling (Idea 21), a positive culture is essential. Here are some tips to get it right:

- Ask the question and give children time to think, jot or talk to a partner before picking a stick.
- Always replace the sticks, so children know they may be asked again.
- Don't use tricks such as colour-coding; if you want to ask a specific child, just ask them! See Idea 21.
- Check often that no sticks are missing.
- Be mindful of your teacher questioning. Random selection is particularly useful for open questions.

Examples
- 'Try this maths question. Do some jottings and compare with your partner. After a few minutes, I'll pick a stick to find out how you've approached it.'
- 'What might happen next? Take a moment to think, then I'll use random selection to find out some of your predictions.'

> **Teaching tip**
>
> If a pupil doesn't respond, you can wait (Idea 14), give time to talk with a partner or rephrase the question. You could also ask 'What are you thinking?' or 'Which bit are you stuck on?', or encourage them to use a talk prompt (Idea 22).

IDEA 21

Cold calling

It's a great way to give the quiet children an opportunity to explain — sometimes they surprise themselves! *Primary teacher*

Purposefully choose who responds, rather than waiting for a volunteer to talk.

Teaching tip

During pair talk, listen out for interesting thoughts and ideas, and invite specific pupils to share these with the class.

Taking it further

Search for 'cold calling' on the 'Teach Like a Champion' website for positive video examples.

'Cold calling' has a number of advantages. All pupils know that you expect them to contribute — it's not optional. Everyone is involved in the learning. It is also a useful way of continually checking for understanding. Cold calling allows you to hear from a range of pupils and to specifically target which children respond to which points.

Good practice for cold calling

- Try to make it warm, not cold! Think about the tone you use, your facial expressions and so on. You want pupils to know that you are genuinely interested in what they are thinking. You also want them to know that you value their partial thinking and that getting a complete answer isn't the only aim. Classroom climate is important. Make sure pupils don't feel picked on.
- Give thinking time, or time to talk with a partner, before you cold call.
- When planning, think about who you might ask specific questions to. Use pupil jottings, written work and previous contributions to inform this.

Be aware — deciding in the moment which pupils to choose can take a lot of energy, so sometimes plan in advance who you will choose. There is also a risk of unconscious bias — be mindful of this. Again, planning can help. Note also that random selection (Idea 20) removes both of these problems.

IDEA 22

No more rabbits in headlights!

They use the prompts to help — it takes away the pressure of answering immediately. Year 4 teacher

Empower pupils to use their voices, even when they aren't sure.

It's useful to provide talk prompts that enable pupils to ask for thinking time or help:
- 'I'm not sure yet.'
- 'Please can I have some time to think?'
- 'Please could you speak a bit louder?'
- 'I'm a bit confused about... Please could you repeat the question?'
- 'Please can I talk to a partner?'
- 'Please could you rephrase the question?'
- 'I'm stuck because...'

These prompts make a huge difference during whole-class talk; pupils can express what they need, rather than panicking. They realise it's OK to say 'I need some help'. This is a cultural change — it changes pupils' status from passive to active learners. They know that we expect them to say something, even if it's to explain that they don't know or don't understand.

- Display the prompts where everyone can see them.
- Give opportunities for pupils to practise using them.
- To make sure everyone has the opportunity to practise asking for help, ask super-challenging questions from time to time.
- Model with an adult, to help normalise the language.

Like many of the prompts in this book, once pupils have had the chance to use them frequently, they will become part of their language and you won't need to keep reminding them.

> **Teaching tip**
>
> If a pupil asks for thinking time or to talk to a partner, go back to them a few moments later, so they do still get that important opportunity of speaking to the class. The prompts are not about providing a way to opt out! Your pupils must know you have high expectations — you want them to express their thinking.

> **Bonus idea** ★
>
> Colour-code the prompts (for example, use coloured speech bubbles around them). If you ask a child a question and they don't respond, say, 'Use one of the yellow talk prompts' or point to the yellow prompts.

IDEA 23

Talking objects

As soon as she had the stone, she started talking! *Year 1 teacher*

Talking objects help pupils to speak up, and help those who sometimes dominate to listen and wait for their turn.

> **Teaching tip**
>
> If your pupils fiddle with the talking objects at first, don't panic. You can get beyond this through training and high expectations. (They could fiddle with pens, but we still use them!)

You can use talking objects to facilitate turn-taking in whole-class talk, group talk or pair talk.

Select some suitable talking objects. For whole-class talk, use a larger object such as a teddy, so that everyone can see it. For group and pair talk, smaller objects such as pebbles or cubes work fine.

Explain to your class: 'When you have the talking cube, it means it's your turn to talk.'

Model, with another adult, passing the object and the quality of talk you are expecting. For example:

Teacher: The first thing we did was check our equipment. (Passes the object)

Additional adult: Then we put the salt into the water. (Passes the object)

Teacher: After that, we...

Talking objects in pairs

Give out one talking object to each pair. Several things often happen:
- The partner who tends to talk more stops talking and passes the object when their partner holds out their hand for it.
- The partner who tends to talk less starts talking when they are given the object.

It's easier to hold out a hand for an object than to interrupt. This can help balance the talk.

When giving out talking objects to pairs, sometimes hand the object to the partner who tends to talk less, so that they speak first.

> **Bonus idea** ★
>
> When doing rounds (Idea 24), use a talking object to make it very clear that everyone will get a turn to talk.

IDEA 24

Rounds

I like it because I get to talk. *Age 8*

A tried-and-trusted way to hear every pupil's voice — make sure you have it in your oracy toolkit.

In a round, everyone has a turn; each child speaks after the person next to them. This has many benefits:
- Pupils who don't volunteer to speak often join in when it's their turn in a round.
- Pupils become used to speaking to the class.
- You hear everyone's voice, ideas and thoughts.
- You can listen fully; you don't have to manage the talk.
- You can assess understanding, and get a snapshot of the depth and range of thinking.

Rounds are straightforward to organise in a circle, but can also be used when pupils are at tables. Some people call this 'Round Robin':
- The first time, introduce it by saying, 'When we do Round Robin, everyone needs to speak. When everyone on a table has spoken, someone on the nearest table starts. Each time we do this, I'll choose someone different to start.'
- Important — the teacher doesn't organise the order! Apart from a short instruction ('Round Robin starting with Joseph'), you won't need to speak until every pupil has had their turn.

Rounds work well when you want pupils to hear lots of different ideas. For example:
- Geography: Why might people migrate?
- Maths: Multiples of five (e.g. 95, 30, 165).

Many talk games work well in rounds (see Ideas 75, 77 and 78).

Teaching tip

Set up your pupils for success by giving time to talk and think in pairs first. Jottings are useful.

Taking it further

Rounds in a class of 30 can be time-consuming, so use word limits sometimes. A limit of three, five or ten words works well. One-word rounds can be as quick as 30 seconds. Rounds with word limits are valuable opportunities for less confident talkers to develop their oracy skills.

IDEA 25

I jot, therefore I talk

It makes me think better. *Age 7*

Get your pupils writing notes for better listening and talk.

> **Taking it further**
>
> Give the jotters a special name to raise their status. For example 'oracy jotters', 'thinking journals' or 'QI books' (Questions and Ideas books).

Provide your class with jotters. Encourage them to jot notes as they learn. This will support talk in several ways:

- It provides thinking time. 'What do you think about what Chloe just said? Make a note.' Or, 'Last week we spoke about alliteration — jot down a few examples.' Or, 'Have a think about that, make some notes, then I'll ask some of you what you are thinking.'
- When pupils have notes, their confidence to talk can dramatically increase. Children who have previously seemed less vocal are more likely to contribute. Or if you randomly select a pupil, they can look at their jottings before speaking or read out what they've written.
- The quality of what a pupil contributes after they've noted their ideas is often much better than if they had said the first thing that came into their head. Everyone's thinking and talking is better.

There are various moments when jotting can be helpful. For example:

- while somebody's talking; as well as helping the note-taker, taking notes is also a way of showing active listening
- as part of thinking time, as above
- during partner talk (see Idea 48).

You could let pupils make all their notes on whiteboards, but then thoughts and ideas will be lost. If they have a jotter, they can refer back.

Jotting often also helps pupils to enjoy writing, because it's free-form and low pressure. (Note — you don't need to mark jotters!)

IDEA 26

Everyone together!

Since we introduced chanting of key knowledge, there's been a marked improvement in attainment. *Year 6 teacher and maths lead*

Speaking out loud all together is active and inclusive — everyone gets involved. It builds confidence to speak, and reinforces key vocabulary and facts quickly.

Three moments to use speaking all together

1 **New vocabulary:** When you teach or come across new words, get pupils to repeat them all together out loud after you. Do this at least three times.

2 **Key facts:** The more times pupils say pieces of key knowledge out loud, the more they will remember them. For example, 'A right angle has 90 degrees.' Say the fact and get pupils to repeat, or have them chorally read out key facts from your slides. Put everything you want them to read in unison in a specific colour, so everyone knows what to do.

3 **Pupil responses:** Get everyone to repeat together what another pupil has said. This has a huge impact on listening and is energising. It works well when you want short contributions such as key words, headlines or concepts.

How to cue it

Choose the cue that you prefer and be consistent. Make sure your cue is clear and simple. For example:
- **Verbal:** 'My turn, your turn.' 'Class!' 'Everyone!' 'All together!' '1-2-3.'
- **Non-verbal:** Click your fingers, point to your ear or open your hands.

Teaching tip

Have high expectations from the first time you do this — if you haven't got everyone joining in, repeat again until everyone does. Investing a bit of time at this stage will save you time later!

Taking it further

Have two non-verbal cues, one that means 'thinking time' (e.g. touch your shoulders) and one that means 'everyone speak' (e.g. open fingers). That way, you can ask a question, give thinking time and then have everyone respond together.

Bonus idea ★

Use singing or chanting when lining up or walking in from lunch.

IDEA 27

What about the 'quiet children'?

Children should be doing more talking so when they talk to others they won't be nervous. You'll get better at it. *Age 7*

Strategies to develop confidence and audibility.

Should we try to get every child to talk? Should we insist on this? Should everybody talk to the class?

The reasons why some children are unconfident or quiet when speaking to the class are complex and varied. And when starting to prioritise oracy and classroom dialogue, teachers sometimes worry that certain pupils will feel nervous, shy, embarrassed or panicky. It can be tempting to allow these pupils to opt out.

However, our responsibility as educators is to create the conditions where these children can have their voices heard, share their opinions and vocalise their ideas. Pupils need support to increase their confidence. We mustn't be too quick to label them as 'shy' or 'quiet'.

Just as in any area of the curriculum, the higher the expectations, the more pupils will achieve. We wouldn't allow children to not stretch in PE or not do times tables in maths!

But just as we wouldn't want anyone to get injured in PE, we don't want to create anxiety around talk. So, we need to approach oracy teaching with sensitivity and support. Developing a nurturing, positive, respectful classroom climate is paramount. Part 1 of this book addresses this in detail.

Within that climate, provide numerous and varied opportunities for everyone to gain

> **Teaching tip**
>
> If you have concerns around selective mutism, get expert advice through your SENDCo. The book *Can I tell you about Selective Mutism?* (Johnson and Wintgens, 2012) is an accessible and helpful reference.

> **Taking it further**
>
> The 'Quiet in the classroom' chapter in *Quiet Power* (Cain, 2016) provides useful further insight.

confidence in talking. You will find many examples throughout this book. Here are eight particularly helpful ones:

Give 'quiet children' **multiple opportunities to speak to the class**. Ask them directly:
- 'Harry, read out the title, please.'
- 'Zeeshan, is that the same or different from how you worked it out?'
- 'Yana, what have you written down?'
- 'What do you think, Tyler?'

You can **plan in advance**, for example, that you're going to ask Harry several times over a couple of weeks to say something to the class. Make sure you do this in a nurturing way. You might be surprised at how rapidly he becomes more confident.

Dedicate time and **opportunities to practise talking**. You could have a weekly or daily talk time. See Idea 91 and 15.

Provide **questions that don't have a single correct answer**. See Idea 16.

Stop using hands up; use alternative **approaches that increase participation**. See Ideas 20, 21 and 60.

Before expecting pupils to speak to the whole class, ensure that you **give time for pair talk, thinking or jotting**. See Part 4 of this book, and Ideas 14 and 25.

Use **talking toys** and do plenty of **rounds**. See Ideas 23 and 24.

Use **talk prompts** and **speaking frames**. These can build confidence, especially if multiple opportunities for oral rehearsal are provided. See Idea 33.

Play lots of **low-pressure, fun, silly talk games**. See Part 8 – lots of these can be done in pairs with an easy topic, just to get everyone talking.

To summarise – if you want to develop children's confidence to talk, make sure you have **high expectations**, prioritise **classroom climate** and provide **opportunities to talk**.

> **Bonus idea** ★
>
> Frequently doing one-word rounds of low-pressure things, such as favourite food, favourite animal or favourite character, can hugely help develop confidence. It gradually becomes normal to speak to the class.

IDEA 28

Please could you speak a bit louder?

It's important, because if they're making a very valid contribution and you can't hear it, that could hinder learning! *Age 11*

If a child is inaudible, encourage other children in the class to respectfully ask them to speak up.

Teaching tip

When you start this approach, if your pupils are not being polite enough, address this immediately. A role play can help. Select two pupils to experiment with different tones of voice and wording and ask the class to reflect on which is the most helpful and appropriate.

Often children can't hear their peers in whole-class talk. This is a missed learning opportunity – all those whispered or mumbled contributions could help others! This technique is a very simple way of improving things.

Next time one of your pupils says something in whole-class talk that you think others can't hear, use this as a chance to take action:

1. Check with the class: 'Raise your hand if you couldn't hear that.'
2. Ask someone sitting on the other side of the room from the speaker to say to them, 'Please could you speak a bit louder?' Be clear that this needs to be said in an extremely polite tone.
3. Tell your class that you want them to always ask classmates to speak louder if they can't hear. Be clear with your expectations: 'I'm not going to tell you who should say "Please speak a bit louder" – I want you all to have the responsibility. If people can't hear, somebody needs to say something.'
4. Tell them that you expect just one of them to make the request. If two pupils make the request at the same time, praise the one who stops: 'Thank you for being respectful – you realised someone else was already speaking.'

IDEA 29

The volumiser

It's made such a difference to the quality of talk in the classroom.
Year 4 teacher

Choose between one and three pupils to have a special job during whole-class talk. Ask them to silently stand up when they can't hear what one of their peers is saying. They are called 'volumisers'.

If one of the volumisers stands, the pupil speaking is expected to say their point again, louder.

Make sure the volumisers are spaced out around the class, near the edges, so that they are covering the whole range of where the sound needs to reach, they are not blocking the view if they stand, and they are clearly visible to all pupils. They do not need to tuck in their chairs – they should stand up carefully and respectfully, with no noise.

This easy, inobtrusive technique helps both the pupils who can't hear and the ones who are practising speaking louder. It does interrupt a pupil's flow of thinking and talking, but it's worth it. A pupil may think they are communicating, yet no one is receiving their message. If we let pupils continually talk quietly, we're not developing their skills.

Pupils enjoy the responsibility of being volumisers and the fact that they are contributing to learning – that everyone can hear what is being said. They like helping the whole class and they like helping individuals to improve their communication skills.

This is about having a classroom of high expectations, where pupil talk is valued as a resource for learning: everyone needs to hear what everyone else is saying. Pass ownership to your pupils!

> **Teaching tip**
>
> As with many of these techniques, if you do them intensively for several weeks or a term, you will reap the benefits – audibility will be much better and you may not need to continue using the technique.

IDEA 30

Cut-ups

It immediately encourages dialogue and collaboration. *Year 6 teacher*

Turn a passive learning moment into an active learning opportunity by asking pupils, in pairs or groups, to sort or rank content using slips of paper.

Teaching tip

Do this in pairs or trios, so everyone is involved. Don't give pupils individual sets of cut-ups to stick in their books, as this will remove the critical element of collaborative talk.

Taking it further

You can also use pictures and objects:

- Sort these foods into 'from plants' and 'from animals'.
- Which of these items would you take on an expedition?
- Order these objects from 'least likely to find at a beach' to 'most likely to find at a beach'.

Bonus idea ★

Search online for 'Diamond Nine template'. This is a nuanced version of ranking.

This can be used in any area of the curriculum:

- Order facts about the Tudors from least disgusting to most disgusting.
- Organise statements about our local area into true and false.
- Sort calculations into correct and mistakes.
- Sort opinions about climate change into agree and disagree.
- Order our ground rules for talk from easiest to most difficult. (See Idea 49.)

Pupils think together, physically moving the cut-up papers into different orders or groups as their discussion develops.

Get into the habit of printing relevant content and cutting it up. You will need one set for each pair or group, so it will take a few minutes. However, it's worth it for these reasons:

- **Participation:** Giving pupils something hands-on as a focus for their talk task means everyone gets involved.
- **Thinking skills:** Tasks like this nurture both collaborative and critical thinking – pupils work together and are motivated to justify their choices and convince their partner.
- **Accountability:** The output is a tangible arrangement of things; this raises responsibility for the learning.
- **Monitoring:** You can make quick visual observations to assess engagement and understanding.

IDEA 31

Contribution counters

Oh, please, Miss! Please can we use the counters again? *Age 10, requesting another chance to practise self-regulating his talk*

Contribution counters develop self-awareness and help us value every voice.

Give everyone two or three counters, which they 'spend' when they speak in the discussion.

This simple device is very powerful. The counters become a physical representation of equality – of equal voice and equal participation.

Contribution counters:
- are empowering – they can be a vehicle for 'less confident talkers' to put their opinions forward
- make 'regular talkers' more self-aware that they sometimes dominate
- help everyone be more inclusive ('I'll pass to Juno – you've not had a turn yet, have you?')
- mean that you as the teacher can easily see who has and hasn't spoken yet ('Jessie, would you like to say something?')
- help us value every voice – show that we want everyone to speak
- encourage children to use every contribution wisely – they have to think things through carefully before they speak
- push children to say more than just the first thing they think of – by being expected to use more than one counter they have to think more deeply.

Use them in whole-class discussions, P4C (Idea 57) or in group talk tasks. Combine them with speaker chooses (Idea 60): 'Look around. Choose someone who still has two counters left.'

Teaching tip

When using contribution counters in a circle, pupils get up and put their counter into the middle when they speak. If you'd rather they weren't moving around, they can simply push their counters forward.

Taking it further

To think further about participation in class discussions, do a tally every now and then of who is talking. Over time, as you implement different strategies, this should change.

Bonus idea ★

Reveal that a colour means a specific challenge: 'Today, yellow counters mean "five words only"! Who has yellow? Great – you all have the challenge of making concise contributions.' (Green counters could become 'question counters' – people with them are responsible for asking questions to clarify or deepen thinking.)

IDEA 32

Jigsaw

A great way to develop oracy skills and deepen learning at the same time! *Alan Howe, Oracy Cambridge*

A fun structure to get everyone talking — pupils start in 'home groups', go to 'expert groups' then report back to their 'home group'.

Teaching tip
Use a timer to ensure that things stay on track.

Taking it further
Jigsaw works best if pupils have to make use of their combined knowledge. Follow Jigsaw with a whole-class discussion to apply new learning, such as 'What is the most fascinating thing about Antarctica?'

Here is how the Jigsaw discussion structure could work in a lesson about Antarctica.

Step 1 Pupils start in 'home groups' of six.
Step 2 Each pupil takes on one aspect: climate, creatures, humans, landscape, resources, conservation.
Step 3 All delegates for each aspect move to sit together. For example, all delegates for 'climate' move to sit together. The new groups are called 'expert groups'.
Step 4 The expert groups have a set time to look at facts, images and information about their aspect of Antarctica. They take turns to read this prepared material together, discuss it, check if they understand it and note down three key points, ready to summarise.
Step 5 Everyone returns to their home group. Each person has two minutes to present to their peers what they found out in their expert group. After each two-minute summary, the rest of the home group has one minute to ask clarification questions.

The magical thing about this structured activity is that every pupil gets to become an expert and teach some of their peers something new. This makes the speaking and listening really purposeful. Jigsaw is great for developing oracy confidence and the skills of summarising, explaining and responding to questions. Use it across the curriculum to deepen learning.

Bonus idea ★
Give talk prompts to help pupils summarise, such as 'I would like to share five key things…'

IDEA 33

Tailored talk prompts

It's really helpful. You can learn quickly if you use the prompts and talk. *Age 9*

Create talk prompts and frames for your lessons to support pupils to speak with confidence about what they're learning. Talking about the learning makes it more memorable.

1 As part of lesson planning, think about what talk prompts or frames would help.
2 Write them on slides or flip charts ready to use.
3 Create opportunities in the lesson for your pupils to use them.

Some examples when learning about volcanoes:

Talk prompts to start the lesson
Something I'm wondering about volcanoes is…
Something that worries me about volcanoes is…
Something I want to know about volcanoes is…

Talk prompts to practise target vocabulary
One thing I know about lava is that…
When a volcano is dormant, it…
When volcanoes erupt…
The crater of the volcano…

Speaking frames
Provide pupils with speaking frames to give opportunities to speak for longer on a subject, and to practise different phrases and language structures. They will benefit from listening first, so show the frame and model using it, adding in details and key vocabulary. Then give them time to practise in pairs before speaking to the whole class.

Example: Volcanoes are… They are located… When they erupt,… Most volcanic eruptions are caused by… A famous volcano is…

> **Teaching tip**
>
> If the prompt contains unfamiliar words or phrases, use oral rehearsal. Say each new word or phrase, and have pupils repeat it out loud in unison at least three times.

> **Bonus idea** ★
>
> Online AI generators can help you create talk prompts for different lessons. As always, use your professional judgement – think critically about which suggested prompts to use.

IDEA 34

Oracy to develop reflective learners

It means you have time to process what you do in the lesson. *Age 9*

Reflection is a key part of learning. Link it to oracy development by providing relevant talk prompts. These will build pupils' capacity to think and talk about their learning.

Teaching tip

Create time for verbal reflections at the end of each day. Select some of these prompts to support this. Vary the talk format. For example, use whole-class discussion with a talking object, partner talk combined with reporting back on partners' opinions, or small groups with contribution counters.

Talking about what I've learned
- I found out that...
- I realised that...
- One thing I discovered was...
- The most important thing I learned was...

Talking about how I feel
- Something I enjoyed in the lesson was...
- Something I found interesting was...
- Something I am proud of is...
- I am wondering...

Talking about peer support
- One of my classmates helped me by...
- I would like my classmates to...

Talking about next steps
- A goal I have for tomorrow is...
- Something I need to practise is...
- Next time I do... I will...

Talking about challenges
- Something I found challenging was...
- Something that frustrated me was...
- I was challenged when...; however...
- A moment I struggled today was when...
- A risk I took was...
- A thinking strategy I used was...

Talking about mistakes
- Mistakes help me...
- A mistake I made today was...
- Something I wish I had done differently was...

Bonus idea ★

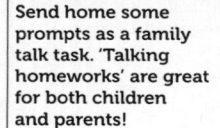

Send home some prompts as a family talk task. 'Talking homeworks' are great for both children and parents!

Part 3

Learning to listen

IDEA 35

Don't expect it to just happen!

Sometimes I start to daydream. I think we should have a bit more time to know how to listen. *Age 7*

Dedicate time to teach listening to your class and give them multiple opportunities to practise.

Teaching tip

Shut the door! Background noise can distract pupils and make it very hard for them to hear each other. Try to reduce it to improve the quality of listening, thinking and talk.

Taking it further

Search online for 'A Minute of Listening' – a wonderful free resource.

Teaching the skill of listening is often neglected. Apart from telling a class or a child to listen, or berating pupils for their lack of listening, it is rarely mentioned. Reminders to listen are not the same as learning to listen!

Children benefit from having time to think about what listening is and how to do it well. Use questions such as these to raise awareness of listening among your learners. As little as a five-minute reflection using one of these questions each week will make a difference.

1. Do you like listening?
2. Who do you know that is a good listener? What makes them a good listener?
3. What do you like more – talking or listening?
4. Which is more important – listening or talking?
5. When is it easy to listen and when is it difficult?
6. How do you know if somebody is listening?
7. How does it feel when someone listens really well?
8. How good a listener are you?
9. What helps you listen better?
10. Why do you sometimes not listen well?
11. Can you think of ten ways to show that you're listening?
12. Good idea/bad idea – doing something at the same time as listening?
13. What do people sometimes do when they should be listening?

14 Is there a difference between respectful listening and active listening?
15 Is there a difference between hearing and listening?

Simple activities to practise listening

Different things Everyone takes turns to say a different thing from a category, e.g. animals. This requires careful listening to know which words have already been said. Use visual prompts, such as a poster of animals. (Combine with jotting to support memory.) Works well in a circle.

Favourite things Everyone takes turns to say their favourite fruit or colour. When everyone has had a go, ask, 'Which colour was the most popular?' or 'Which fruit did nobody say?'. Questions such as these motivate careful listening.

Copy games Clapping rhythm games are great for practising close listening. Also try 'repeat after me' chants and songs, where the challenge is not just to repeat what you say but how you say it – for example, quiet voice, robot voice and so on. Look online for 'call and repeat' songs such as Boom Chicka Boom.

Games that encourage children to make connections or say whether they agree or disagree are also excellent for developing listening. (See Ideas 73, 74 and 78.)

> **Bonus idea** ★
>
> Talk to your class in a very quiet voice sometimes. This encourages close listening. You can also play a 'whisper challenge' game where you tell the class specific things to do, in a very quiet voice: 'Tap the desk with your little finger', 'Put your thumb on your chin.'

Listening instructions Give specific listening instructions before a task. Simply knowing what you're listening out for makes it much more tangible:

Instead of saying	Try saying
Remember to listen.	Listen out for and jot key words.
I'm going to play you an audio clip about life in Victorian times. Listen carefully.	I'm going to play you an audio clip about life in Victorian times. Listen out for three things that you think sound horrible!

IDEA 36

Reduce repetition

When he repeats I get bored 'cos I've already heard it. I just have to sit there listening. Age 8

If you stop repeating, their listening will dramatically improve.

Teaching tip

Don't repeat instructions! Say things once only. If you give instructions many times, the impact can be that your pupils don't listen carefully. If there is a need to repeat, ask a child to do it.

Many teachers have a habit of repeating pupil answers and explanations. There are several reasons why, including fear of awkward silences, making sure everyone can hear, thinking aloud and improving the clarity of the child's point. However, if adults repeat all pupil talk, it can devalue pupil talk, reduce pupil listening and lower expectations that pupils will respond audibly. It also means that there is a lot of teacher talk — which pupils may tune out of — and less opportunity for quiet thinking time.

When pupils know that their teacher does not repeat, they learn to listen closely. So, whenever you're tempted to repeat a response, try doing one of these things instead.

- If you feel that someone needs to hear the response again, ask a pupil to repeat it.
- If you feel that everyone would benefit from some time to process the child's point, allow some silent thinking time.
- If it was a particularly important idea or piece of information, make that clear: 'That's a very important point. Danny, can you repeat what Ibrahim has just said so we can all hear it again?' (See Idea 40 — this is not about catching Danny out.)

Audibility

If the pupil wasn't loud enough for everyone to hear, invest time in addressing audibility in your classroom. Make sure you have a clear expectation that everyone listens to all that has been said in whole-class talk — not just the teacher! (See Ideas 28 and 29.)

IDEA 37

What does bad listening look like?

It feels discouraging and annoying! *Age 11*

Use the power of role play to highlight common problems.

Model with another adult, or a child who can cope with a challenge. Ask them to tell you something about their hobbies. When they start talking, deliberately show some bad listening behaviours. For example:
- Look out of the window.
- Make distracting movements or be restless.
- Yawn, hum or sigh.

Stop after around 30 seconds. Invite a pupil to ask your partner how they felt: 'Marko, please will you ask Sir how he felt during that conversation.'

Marko: How did you feel, Sir?
Sir: Well, I felt a bit upset because I didn't think Ms Page was listening to me. I felt ignored.

Now ask your class to think about how the listening could be better. They might come up with ideas like face the person, nod, show encouraging facial expressions, make interested or empathetic noises, offer appropriate comments or questions.

Repeat the role play using their ideas. Get Marko to ask again how Sir felt. There should be a big difference!

Point out that showing active listening is not only important one to one (where it's more obvious) but also during group and whole-class talk.

Taking it further

Give pupils opportunities to do their own role plays of bad and good listening in pairs. This experience is a powerful way to help them empathise with the speaker.

Bonus idea ★

With your class, create a list or annotated poster of what good listening looks like.

IDEA 38

Look at the speaker

We do it to show mutual respect to each other. *Age 8*

Giving attention to the speaker is an important aspect of active listening.

Teaching tip

Be aware that you may come across pupils whose additional needs or cultural background mean that they are uncomfortable looking directly at the speaker. As with any situation like this, be sensitive and adapt accordingly.

Taking it further

Initially, the simple instruction 'Look at the speaker' is very helpful. However, there are other ways of giving attention, and it's worth discussing these and trying them out. For example, making notes about what's being said, turning your body towards the speaker, or showing respect by being still and focused. You can also encourage pupils to show they're listening by nodding in agreement or putting their thumbs up when they agree with what is being said.

Most pupils are used to the idea of looking at the speaker when the teacher is the speaker. Make sure they give the same level of attention when their classmates speak. As well as improving listening, this will impact positively on speakers' self-esteem.

During whole-class talk, ask your pupils to give attention to the speaker. It's a way of showing them support and that you're interested in what they are saying. This is an important social skill.

Use reminders such as:
- 'Let's all look at Owen now – he is the speaker.'
- 'Let's all remember to look at the speaker, to show we're listening.'

If children feel a little uncomfortable at first, don't worry. They will soon get used to it and their confidence will grow. Remember that speaking to an audience is an important life skill and being the centre of attention for a few moments is part of this.

Practise until giving attention to the speaker becomes a normal and embedded part of your classroom culture.

IDEA 39

Check your class

We say their name! It's very helpful – if people are zoning out it's a good way to get their attention. *Age 10*

This is a simple technique that you can empower your pupils to use in whole-class talk. The idea is that they check their peers are focused on them before they start speaking.

1. Next time a pupil is about to say something in whole-class talk, say: 'Wait a moment, Zack. Have a check that everyone's showing you respectful listening.'
2. Zack should then look around the room to check that everyone is ready.
3. Then say to Zack: 'If you see anyone that isn't ready, you can politely say their name.'

Zack now has permission to politely remind his classmates to give respectful attention. Once you do this a few times, your pupils will realise that you expect them to always pause momentarily and check before speaking.

Use these words to gently prompt when needed: 'Check your class before you speak.'

The impact of this small intervention is huge:

- Pupil talk immediately gains status. Pupils realise their contributions are a central part of the learning.
- Pupils feel empowered. They have ownership of the learning. They realise they are responsible for making sure everyone hears what they say.
- Pupil audibility improves. Pupils realise their peers need to hear what they say, so they talk more loudly and clearly.
- Pupils become more skilled at speaking to a room full of people. For example, they develop self-confidence, they get used to making eye contact and they notice the reactions of their audience.

Teaching tip

This technique shouldn't interrupt the flow of learning. Once pupils have had opportunities to practise it, it will only take a matter of seconds – a few seconds well spent.

Bonus idea ★

This works well with Stand up to speak up (Idea 62). After standing, encourage the speaker to take a moment to compose themselves – and then check their class.

IDEA 40

What do you think about what Janie said?

It keeps them on their toes. *Year 1 teacher*

Pupil contributions in lessons are a valuable resource for learning, therefore it's vital that everyone is listening to each other. Use these three approaches and see the impact.

Teaching tip

These moves are *not* about catching out pupils who are off-task. They are about creating a positive culture where pupil-to-pupil listening is viewed by all as an essential part of learning.

Taking it further

Target three children each week to develop their listening. Ask them frequently to repeat, or comment on what a classmate has said.

1. Get them to repeat

Expect your pupils to listen closely and be able to repeat what peers say. Be transparent about this: 'I want you all to become excellent listeners so I'll often ask you to repeat what others are saying.'

Try saying, 'Fold your arms if you can repeat what Sol said.' Your class will know that you expect them *all* to fold their arms because you expect everyone to be listening!

2. What do you think about what Janie said?

Imagine a class who constantly reflect and build on each others' contributions. To achieve this, ask pupils what they think about what a classmate has said. For example, 'Holly, what do you think about what Janie said?'

This also impacts positively on the speaker – they know that people have really listened to and engaged with what they said.

3. Has anyone got a different idea?

This move helps children listen to others' ideas and reflect on their own thinking before they speak. It makes it clear that repeated ideas are not required. It also encourages divergent thinking and welcomes different perspectives.

As always, start by seeking responses from a range of pupils via cold call, random selection or speaker chooses. Then ask for additional ideas: 'Has anyone got a different idea?'

IDEA 41

Talk towers

This really motivates them to listen closely to each other!
Year 3 teacher

A common problem in whole-class talk is pupils not listening to each other, and time being wasted by repeated or irrelevant comments. Talk towers promotes quality dialogue by encouraging children to listen and connect to what the previous person has said.

Use talk towers when your class are talking about a big question, such as 'Was life more exciting in Viking times?'. Set expectations: 'In our discussion, I want you to practise making points that connect directly to the previous point.'

Provide a tray of connecting bricks or cubes. The first pupil makes their point and places a brick in the centre of the circle. When the next pupil makes their connecting point, they join on another brick. After several connecting contributions, a tower starts to form. If someone changes to a new idea, they will have to start a new tower.

For example, discussing 'What is art?':
Maria: Art is drawing and painting whatever you feel! (Places her brick in the middle.)
Ava: I agree, art helps people express themselves. (Joins her brick on top of Maria's.)
Thomas: Yes, it's about feelings, and also about telling the world what you think.
Teacher: OK, so you're building on this idea of feelings. Join your brick onto the tower.
Kwame: Art isn't just about painting and drawing. What about sculpture? We saw sculptures in the museum!
Teacher: Good distinction. Let's start a new tower about types of art. OK, Emily, which tower do you want to connect with?

Teaching tip

Label the towers with sticky notes, showing the main concepts. This helps track the dialogue.

Bonus idea ★

To support this approach, provide talk prompts for expanding or building on (see Idea 18).

IDEA 42

How do we know they are listening?

If you don't check that they're listening, it's all pointless. *Phase leader*

Look for clues and evidence that your class are really listening to each other.

When pupils are discussing something in pairs, groups or as a whole class, look for evidence that they are definitely listening to each other. We all know it's possible to give the illusion that we're listening!

Five signs of listening

Use of collaborative talk phrases — for example:

- Supporting or agreeing: 'I want to support Evan's point because...', 'I agree with Kyle's idea.'
- Challenging or disagreeing: 'I disagree with Giorgio because...', 'That's interesting, but...'
- Connecting: 'I'd like to build on what Aisha said...'
- Referring back to what someone has said: 'I'd like to go back to what Dilys said earlier...'
- Asking each other questions: 'What do you think, Rebecca?', 'What did you mean when you said "obscure", Frankie?'

Pupils changing their thinking as a result of dialogue.

Note-taking while peers are talking, and pupils referring to their notes in the dialogue or in their subsequent written work (see Idea 25).

Use of hand signals to connect, question or challenge (see Idea 11).

Pupils reporting what a partner has said (see Idea 48).

Teaching tip

Beware — pupils may use collaborative talk phrases but not actually connect to a previous contribution! For example, they might say 'I'd like to build on...' but then make an unrelated point. So yes, the phrases are a clue, but remember to also listen to the content, to confirm that they've really been listening and thinking about each other's points.

Talking in pairs

Part 4

IDEA 43

What makes a good talk partner?

They always listen to my ideas, not just talk about their ideas. If I don't get it, they say 'Oh, what about this?' Age 9

Ask your class what they think are the key characteristics of a good talk partner.

Discuss with your class what they think a good talk partner does. They could write down a list in pairs, or you could scribe. They might say things like: 'A good talk partner...
- turns to face you
- looks interested
- asks you questions
- gives you time to think
- stays on task
- doesn't take over – gives you time to talk
- thinks about who will talk first
- challenges both of you to go deeper and extend your learning.'

Their responses can be developed into a class checklist or poster for good talk partner behaviours.

As well as helping pupils to reflect on their own behaviours, this process also means that everyone is clear about what they can expect from their partner.

To go deeper, ask your class, 'What makes a bad talk partner?' For example, not listening, interrupting, saying off-task comments, asking irrelevant questions and so on. Make sure they focus on behaviours, not individual children. Or role play with another adult what a 'bad' talk partner would do, and ask your pupils what they noticed. Finish by modelling what a good talk partner would do and then give everyone an opportunity to practise.

> **Bonus idea** ★
>
> Take photos of pairs of pupils in your class showing positive talk partner behaviours – eye contact, facing partner, positive body language, looking interested. Show these before talk partner activities as quick visual reminders.

IDEA 44

Set them up for success

It made such a difference when I modelled the partner talk. Suddenly they all knew what was expected of them! *Year 3 ECT*

There's a lot more to successful pair talk than saying 'Have a chat with your partner'.

When you ask your class to talk in pairs:

Model the type of talk you want to see. If you want them to use target vocabulary or to question each other, model it first with a TA or pupil.

Always check that everyone has a partner —often somebody has popped out to read or gone to an appointment and one child is left with no partner.

Give them something worthwhile to talk about. Make sure the task is meaningful and will impact on learning. Take time to plan interesting and challenging talk tasks.

Give clear and precise instructions

Instead of	Try saying
Have a chat with your partner.	Find out which method your partner prefers and why.
Discuss equivalent fractions with your talk partner.	Discuss with your partner and jot down at least two fractions that are equivalent to ½.
Talk to your partner about the story.	Tell your partner who your favourite character is and why.

Teaching tip

Invest time in making sure your pupils respond quickly to your stop signal.

Bonus idea ★

A simple way of organising partners is 'magnet hands'. If pupils are sitting in a circle, say, 'Magnet hands, starting with Lewis and Abdul.' Lewis and Abdul, who are sitting next to each other, raise one hand each into a high-five and hold it. The pair next to them does the same. The rest of the class gradually discover who their partner is, as the 'magnet hands wave' goes around the circle.

For younger children, 'double magnet hands' works well, as it helps them to remember to turn their body towards their partner.

IDEA 45

Who's first?

Partner 1, tell Partner 2 something they need to remember.
Year 2 teacher

Make sure they know which partner will talk first.

Think about talk partner tasks in your class. Have you noticed problems like these?

- In some pairs, both partners speak at the same time as each other.
- In some pairs, no one speaks.
- In some pairs, the more confident partner dominates.

The following techniques address these issues.

Option 1
Simply make it clear who starts. For example:
'In your pairs, decide who is A and who is B.'
Pause for them to decide.
'OK – Partner A, you talk first.'

Option 2
Do a structured task where you tell them when to swap. For example:
'Partner A, you have one minute to explain to B which subtraction method you prefer and why.'
'Partner B, you now have one minute to ask A clarification questions.'

If you use sequential partner names, such as A and B, it's sometimes worth instructing B to start, as the 'louder' pupil will invariably have decided they are A! Starting with B means the 'quieter' pupil will get a go at speaking first. Names without an obvious hierarchy can also address this. For example, one partner is Brilliant and the other is Fantastic.

Another benefit of having partners named is that it simplifies instructions to change partners. For example: 'Partner B – stand up, and move to sit with a different person.'

Teaching tip

After asking pupils to decide who is A and B, take a moment to check: '"A"s – put your hands on your shoulders.' This extra step is worth it, as often there's someone who missed the instruction or a pair who both insist they are 'A'!

Taking it further

Instruct pupils to decide silently who is Partner 1 and who is Partner 2 by holding up the appropriate number of fingers. Once they're used to this, it's beautifully quick and calm.

IDEA 46

Changing partners

I like talking to different people! Once I had someone who just sat there for a whole term... *Age 5*

Instead of allocating talk partners for the term or half-term, create frequent opportunities for pupils to talk to different people.

Regularly change pairings in your class. You could start by changing them every week; eventually you might change them multiple times in a day.

Benefits of changing talk partners

Talk skills: Pupils gain experience of speaking and listening to people with different accents, vocabulary and ways of saying things.

Social skills and relationships: Pupils get to know each other, help others and communicate with lots of different people.

Positive impact on learning: Different people have different ideas, perspectives and ways of explaining things.

More enjoyable learning: It's interesting to interact with lots of people, and no one gets stuck with someone they don't get on with.

Here are two good ways to select new pairings:
1. **Random**. Cut 15 postcards in half and give them out. Pupils pair up with the person who has the other half of their picture. Pupils like the fairness of this. Online random selectors are also an option.
2. **Targeted**. In specific lessons, for certain tasks, pupils can benefit from carefully chosen pairings. For example, if Elodie is strong at spelling but struggles with accurate punctuation and Mina is strong at punctuation but weak at spelling, they will be able to support each other in their target areas.

> **Teaching tip**
>
> Initially, just do short activities with new partners, to help them get used to working with lots of different people. Once your class are used to changing partners frequently, they won't make a fuss.

> **Bonus idea** ★
>
> Concentric circles: Organise your class into two circles – an inner circle and an outer circle, facing each other in pairs. When you shake a tambourine the outer circle moves around to their next talk partner. This is fun, and great for getting everyone talking to lots of partners in a short space of time.

IDEA 47

Talk prompts for talk partners

They used to just sit there, or complain to me that their partner wasn't talking, but now they're responsible and sort it out themselves! Year 1 teacher

Provide written prompts specifically for talk tasks in pairs.

Teaching tip

Have high expectations: 'Remember, I want you to use the talk partner prompts. I'll be listening out for them!'

Taking it further

Make time for reflection. Ask your class some of these questions: 'Did you find the talk partner prompts easy to use?', 'Which ones were tricky?', 'What impact did they have on your talk?', 'Which other prompts might be useful when we do talk partner tasks?'

Sometimes when we ask pupils to talk in pairs, one of them might dominate the conversation, or one of them might not say much. Talk prompts can help to address this.

Start with a few simple phrases such as these:
- What do you think?
- How do you know?
- It's your turn.
- It's my turn now.

These prompts could be displayed where everyone can see them, or they could be on tables – one per pair.

Build up to more advanced phrases:
- What is your opinion?
- What's your evidence?
- I'm not sure what you mean – can you tell me in a different way?
- Let's focus on what we've been asked to do.

Another problem that sometimes occurs is that pairs finish talking and wait for the next teacher instruction, having done just a minimum amount of talking. Prompts help them to challenge each other to keep thinking, and to think more deeply:
- Can you think of any more examples?
- Let's try to add a bit more detail.
- Let's try to think of a few more reasons.
- Is that definitely true?
- OK – let's summarise what we're thinking.

IDEA 48

Make sure they're on task!

Do you want me to plait your hair? Age 8, during pair talk task

Use these techniques and structures to ensure that partner talk is accountable talk. This will help pupils to focus and stay on task.

Random selection after partner talk
'Do your talk task and then I'll pick a stick.' If you allow time for oral rehearsal with a partner, your pupils will be prepared and confident to speak when they are selected. Set them up for success. This is not about catching children out.

Reporting on what a partner thinks
Let them know in advance that you want them to listen as well as talk: 'In a moment, I'll ask some of you what your partner thinks.' Before you ask someone to report, check whether anyone needs more time to find out what their partner thinks.

Use jottings
Make note-taking an expectation during partner talk. Give specific instructions to encourage this:
- 'Talk to your partner and jot down at least five adjectives together.'
- 'With your partner, make a note of four observations.'

Note – one whiteboard per pair promotes collaborative talk.

Check
Take a moment to stand back and check your pupils. Ask yourself – are they on task? Is this the productive talk I was hoping for? If they're not meeting your expectations, stop them straight away. Reiterate expectations, model the task if needed, then start them off again.

> **Teaching tip**
>
> When your class are doing a talk partner task, watch them carefully. Listen for points that could contribute to the learning. Resist the temptation to join in with one particular pair.

> **Bonus idea** ★
>
> Use thinking structures to encourage accountability. See Idea 84, and search online for 'Double Bubble thinking map'.

Talking in small groups

Part 5

IDEA 49

Ground rules

They're really good, because everyone was shouting out before! *Age 10*

Ground rules for talk are a game-changer in groupwork. They are most effective when developed by children, rather than imposed on them.

> **Teaching tip**
>
> Always display the class ground rules throughout talk tasks. Draw attention to them, and build in time to reflect: 'Are they working?', 'Do they need to be revised?', 'Which of our ground rules is the most important?'

Start by asking your class for ideas: 'I want you to come up with some rules for discussion in groups. With your partner, write down three ideas.' Then show pupils some example rules to consider together. You can also show them the research below – is there anything they would like to include from this? (Pupils may need extra guidance from you to ensure their ground rules cover all important aspects.)

Research
Professor Neil Mercer studied classroom conversations. He found that in good discussions, pupils:
- share relevant information
- engage critically but constructively with each other's ideas
- give reasons for their ideas
- all actively participate
- check understanding by asking questions
- build on each other's responses
- strive for agreement.

Possible ground rules
- We give everyone a chance to talk.
- We consider everyone's ideas carefully.
- We ask everyone: 'What do you think?', 'Why do you think that?'
- We look at and listen to the person talking.
- We give reasons.
- We ask questions.
- We suggest alternative ideas.
- We ask each other for clarification.
- We challenge each other to think deeper.

> **Bonus idea** ★
>
> For some helpful resources, search online for 'discussion guidelines Oracy Cambridge'.

IDEA 50

Exploratory talk

They recognise that classmates are a valuable resource for new thinking. *Lyn Dawes, Oracy Cambridge*

In group talk tasks, we want pupils to listen to each other's reasons, question each other and try to solve things together. However, if we don't teach children how to work well in groups, this is unlikely to happen.

Exploratory talk is a term that describes positive and productive groupwork. It was first introduced by Douglas Barnes and has been established more widely by Neil Mercer.

In exploratory talk, children listen to each other; they think aloud together to make sense of things. They share thoughts that aren't fully formed, take risks and test out ideas in a collaborative atmosphere of trust and support.

Steps you can take to help your pupils become skilled in exploratory talk:
1 Use a whole-class discussion to raise children's awareness of how they currently talk together: 'How is it when you talk in groups? Is it going well? What problems occur?'
2 Support them to list criteria for an effective discussion (see Idea 51).
3 Convert these criteria into a set of 'ground rules' (see Idea 49).
4 Your class should now be ready to try groupwork using exploratory talk. Give them some purposeful talk tasks to practise. (You could use Idea 53.)
5 Get pupils to use their ground rules to reflect on their talk: 'How did you get on with listening to each other?' 'Did you hear anyone say "What do you think?"' 'Which ground rules did you find challenging?'

Teaching tip

Pupils' talk skills will develop the more they do exploratory talk. It's essential that you support them, particularly at first. They will need frequent opportunities to revisit the ground rules and reflect on the quality of their talk.

Taking it further

Going forward, when pupils are discussing in groups, expect and promote exploratory talk. This will impact on learning across the curriculum.

IDEA 51

Bad discussion/good discussion?

It changed everything... Suddenly they were really listening to each other! Year 4 teacher

Sometimes, to get what we want, it helps to think about what we don't want.

Raising awareness about discussion is an important step towards high-quality, productive groupwork (see Idea 50).

Ask your pupils what a **bad** discussion would look like and sound like. They will probably come up with ideas such as: 'People talk at the same time', 'It sometimes gets too noisy', 'Not everyone joins in', 'Sometimes people talk about other things or mess around' and 'Everyone starts arguing'.

Then ask them what a **good** discussion would look like and sound like. Compile a list of their thoughts. It will probably look something like this:

- People listen to each other.
- Everyone is respectful.
- We don't interrupt.
- We take it in turns.
- We don't shout.
- We stay focused.
- People ask sensible questions.

Your class can now use their list as a checklist for their learning talk in groups, or as the starting point for creating some ground rules for talk (see Idea 49).

Teaching tip

Keep groups small for group talk tasks. In large groups it's difficult to ensure everyone's voice is heard. Trios are an effective starting point. Only when your pupils are skilled at group discussion should you gradually increase group size. You may want to start by allocating roles so that everyone knows what they need to do (see Idea 52).

Bonus idea ★

Sometimes, when pupils are talking collaboratively in small groups, allocate one pupil per group the special role of 'Questioner'. Their job is to ask questions to their group to get everyone thinking. This will help develop productive discussion.

IDEA 52

Discussion roles

It's much easier to take part in a discussion if you know exactly what your role is. *Wendy Lee, speech and language therapist*

There are many ways of talking and behaving in groups, and sometimes we get stuck with habits that are limiting. Trying out different roles can be an enlightening experience.

By taking on different roles, pupils realise that successful group talk involves all sorts of techniques. Once your class have gained awareness and skills, they'll habitually use aspects of the different roles to become effective, well-rounded group talkers.

Possible roles:

Encourager: Supports others and encourages them to say more and explain their thoughts. Makes sure everyone's voice is heard and valued. 'That's an interesting point, Theo. Tell us a bit more.' 'What do you think, Lulu?'

Agitator: Pushes the thinking further by introducing different perspectives. Asks challenging questions to help the group to think more deeply. 'Is that always true?', 'What about...', 'What if...'

Scribe: Listens closely and jots the main ideas. Asks for clarification when needed. 'Please can you repeat your point – I didn't get exactly what you meant.'

Spokesperson: Reports the group's main ideas. Listens carefully. Reads what the scribe is writing. Checks and clarifies with the group before speaking. 'Would you agree that our main conclusion is...?'

Manager: Makes sure the task gets completed to the best of the group's ability. May need to refocus them and remind them of the task.

> **Teaching tip**
>
> Make sure pupils take on different roles over time – they can be randomly allocated or targeted, to ensure skill development.

> **Bonus idea** ★
>
> Search online for 'Voice 21's Student Talk Tactics' resource.

IDEA 53

Talking points

It's made them think beyond the obvious. They had a lot of misconceptions at first but they worked it out themselves – they argued with evidence. Year 1 teacher

In this approach, developed by Lyn Dawes, instead of being given questions, pupils are given thought-provoking statements to discuss in small groups. Children spend time exploring these talking points and discovering what they and their group think.

Teaching tip

Make sure your class have good discussion habits: they need to be skilled in exploratory talk (Idea 50) and to have relevant ground rules (Idea 49).

Taking it further

Read *Talking Points: Discussion Activities in the Primary Classroom* by Lyn Dawes (2011). This will give you lots more ideas, techniques and examples to really get your class learning through talking points.

Talking points:
- are statements not questions
- are provocative and interesting
- should be easy to read so that everyone can access them
- give an opportunity to discuss and apply new vocabulary
- help test out thinking and develop reasoning
- can be planned across the curriculum for learning through talk.

Talking points may or may not have a correct answer; where there is one (for example, in maths or science), the value is in how the group works things out together and explains to one another, creating cognitive connections and memorable learning.

To introduce talking points to your class:
- Give out or display some talking points. Number them so pupils can easily refer to them in their discussions.
- Give some discussion prompts that encourage children to listen carefully, share their reasons and question each other.
- Make up talking points for different areas of the curriculum, to promote meaningful dialogue.
- Refresh your own subject knowledge so that you're ready to navigate any pupil misconceptions!

Example 1: Talking points about Goldilocks

Talk together about these statements. Do you agree or disagree? Remember to give reasons.

a) Goldilocks is a nice girl.
b) Goldilocks was naughty.
c) Goldilocks was adventurous.
d) It is never OK to go into a house without permission.
e) Breaking something is OK if it's an accident.

Example 2: Talking points about the air

Think together and share your ideas. Are these true or false? Are there any that you are unsure about? Can you come to an agreement?

a) Air is made of lots of invisible gases.
b) The air is mainly oxygen.
c) We only breathe in oxygen.
d) We breathe out carbon dioxide.
e) Carbon dioxide is a dangerous gas.

Example 3: Talking points about 2D and 3D shapes

How far do you agree or disagree about these statements? Discuss everyone's suggestions. Share your reasons. What conclusions do you come to? Be ready to explain.

a) If the angles of a triangle are all equal, the sides have to be equal too.
b) Irregular polygons have sides of different lengths.
c) There is more than one 3D shape that has no edges or vertices.
d) We can name some quadrilaterals that have no parallel sides.
e) A degree is always a unit that measures angle.

Once pupils have gained good learning habits of thinking together, they will be able to sustain a meaningful and relevant discussion about just one talking point for a considerable time. This is because they will test out ideas together, check for assumptions and exceptions, and challenge each other to think more deeply.

> **Teaching tip**
>
> When pupils first try the talking points approach, always give them a series of statements to discuss (as in the examples). This way, even if they rush through them, they still have plenty of relevant material to discuss.

> **Bonus idea** ★
>
> Whole-class talk after talking points group tasks will not only bring a level of accountability, but can be a useful opportunity for pupils to gain further insights, and to reflect on the quality of their discussions. Ask them: 'Did you enjoy talking together?', 'How did you handle disagreement in your group?', 'What impact did thinking together have on your learning?'

IDEA 54

Placemat consensus

They can't just sit back, but they're not put on the spot. It gets them to talk to each other and listen to each other. *Year 5 ECT*

Placemat consensus is a way to explore concepts and key vocabulary across the curriculum. It supports children to move from individual to collaborative thinking.

Teaching tip

Use placemat consensus to explore a range of concepts, such as conquest in history, habitat in science or worship in RE.

Taking it further

Display prompts to encourage collaborative talk. For example, during Steps 3 and 4: 'What do you mean by...?', 'I'm not sure I understand...', 'I don't completely agree with...'. During Step 6: 'How shall I put...?', 'Does this sound OK?', 'How about...?'

Bonus idea ★

At the end of the activity, a speaker from each group practises reading out the agreed definition. Their groupmates give them constructive feedback such as 'Try speaking a little more slowly' or 'It was great that you made eye contact!' Speakers then take turns to stand and present to the class.

Here's how a placement consensus activity about sustainability would go:

Pupils sit in groups of four with one sticky note each and a blank sheet of paper in the middle.

Step 1 Pupils independently write what they think sustainability is on their sticky note.
Step 2 Pupils take turns to read what they wrote and place their sticky note onto a different corner of the blank paper.
Step 3 Pupils clarify and question each other's ideas.
Step 4 Pupils think together to work out how to collectively explain the concept of sustainability.
Step 5 Each group agrees who will scribe.
Step 6 All pupils support the scribe to write the group's agreed final explanation of sustainability in the centre of the paper.

This structured approach means everyone thinks, and everyone talks. Physically placing the sticky note helps with turn-taking. Pupils work collaboratively, use each other's ideas and gain greater understanding.

Think carefully about groupings. Sometimes, grouping pupils with similar levels of understanding can result in higher-quality dialogue. As always, remember to give pupils opportunities to work with different people over time (see Idea 46).

Whole-class talk

Part 6

IDEA 55

Dialogue

Dialogue is essential to the meaningful development of knowledge. It is also essential to becoming a better citizen and a better human being. *Neil Phillipson, 21st Century Learners*

Classroom dialogue makes teaching and learning exciting, enjoyable and more effective. There's no longer a sole focus on getting 'the right answer'.

Dialogue, put simply, is thinking together. It's a collaborative search for understanding and meaning and there is plenty of evidence that it has a profound impact on learning.

Of course, dialogue isn't always appropriate: there are times when the best approach is teacher instruction — about key knowledge or a new method, perhaps. But ideally, children will experience a balance of instruction and dialogue.

Dialogue helps children to make connections, question assumptions, give reasons and evidence, appreciate other perspectives and feel heard. Dialogue also helps teachers to be aware of what children do and don't understand, and build better relationships with their pupils. This approach is sometimes called 'dialogic teaching'.

Many of the ideas in this book are about dialogic teaching and learning. But here are some pointers:

Mindset
- The number one building block is to think of pupil talk as a resource for learning.
- Instead of you doing all the explaining, get pupils to work hard explaining to each other.
- See misconceptions and alternative perspectives as opportunities. Value them.

> **Teaching tip**
> Take a seat: Sit down at the side of the room to signal that you want pupils to discuss with each other.

> **Taking it further**
> Check out Robin Alexander's extensive work on classroom dialogue. See *A Dialogic Teaching Companion* (2020) for the most recent version of his framework for dialogic teaching.

- Welcome questions – they encourage pupil curiosity and give you insight into their thinking.
- Make it clear that pupils should be listening closely and continually evaluating what their peers say – asking themselves constantly do they agree or disagree?
- Practise listening deeply and seeking to understand the pupil (see Idea 5).

Start to create a dialogic classroom
- Plan challenging, open-ended tasks and questions. These don't have to be complicated – for example, in English you might use a question such as 'Which character made the best choices?'
- Model good listening. Listen closely to each contribution and welcome thinking even if it isn't complete (see Idea 4). Encourage and challenge pupils to listen deeply to each other: 'Elijah, please will you summarise the main points.'
- Encourage pupils to elaborate, explain, and consider carefully what others are saying (see Idea 56).
- Encourage pupils to look at and speak to each other. Consider classroom layout.
- Notice and praise active listening and different types of thinking: 'Super justification, Shania!'
- Provide prompts and scaffolds to give pupils language of dialogue – for example, to agree and disagree (see Idea 18).
- Allow plenty of thinking time.
- Resist speaking after every pupil. You don't need to evaluate everything they say – other members of the class can do that.
- Spot opportunities to relate learning to your pupils' experiences and concerns.
- Establish ground rules (see Ideas 49 and 90).

> **Teaching tip**
>
> Brush up on your subject knowledge so you are ready to ask relevant questions, responding to what your pupils say. This is essential and will give you the confidence and ability to facilitate dialogue successfully. If you realise you aren't up to speed, stop. Don't just let pupils continue to make random or flawed contributions! 'I need to check some facts. Let's come back to this tomorrow.' Or 'OK, everyone, a homework challenge for you – is a turtle a reptile?'

> **Bonus idea** ★
>
> **Last three to speak: Part-way through a discussion, pause it and ask pupils to remember the last three speakers: 'What did they say? What reasons did they give? Do you agree or disagree with what they said? Discuss this with your partner.' This is a simple way to improve listening and deepen dialogue.**

IDEA 56

Teacher talk moves

Moves that encourage students to elaborate their own and each other's ideas have particular potency. *Robin Alexander*

Use moves from the numbered list below to make your teacher talk more effective, increase the amount and quality of pupil talk, add challenge and generate valuable classroom dialogue.

> **Teaching tip**
>
> These talk moves are very simple. The skill is judging when to use them, and turning them into a habit for yourself. When said in an encouraging, positive tone and used as a core part of your teaching, they will transform learning. (See also Part 1.)

These are moves that Catherine O'Connor and Sarah Michaels observed in the classrooms of teachers who had mastered the art of facilitating inclusive and productive discussions.

To get started, ask yourself these reflection questions:
- Looking at the four goals listed below, which is the current priority for your learners?
- Do you already do any of the talk moves? If you already do some, do you do them naturally or on purpose? Which do you rarely do?
- Which will your pupils find most challenging?
- Think again about your priority goal. Which move will you add to your practice immediately? When will you use it? How will you remember?

Goal: Help children share, expand and clarify their own thinking

1. **Time to think:** As well as silent thinking time, use pair talk and writing as think time.
2. **Say more:** 'Go on…', 'Tell us more', 'Say a bit more about that', 'Can you give an example?'
3. **So, are you saying…?:** 'So, let me see if I've got what you're saying. Are you saying…?' Always leave space for the child to agree or disagree and say more.

Goal: Help children listen carefully to each other

4. **Who can rephrase or repeat?:** 'Who can repeat what Maya just said, or put it into their own words?', 'What did your partner say?' After a classmate repeats or rephrases, check with the original pupil: 'Is that what you meant?'

Goal: Help children deepen their reasoning

5. **Ask for evidence or reasoning:** 'How do you know?', 'Why do you think that?', 'What's your evidence?', 'How did you arrive at that conclusion?'
6. **Challenge or counter-example:** 'Does it always work that way?', 'How does that idea fit with David's example?'

Goal: Help children think with others

7. **Agree/disagree:** 'Do you agree or disagree? (And why?)', 'What do people think about what Cleo said?'
8. **Add on:** 'Can you add onto the idea that Rhian is building?', 'Paddy, can you take that further?'

Examples

When children explain to the class how they worked out a maths problem, the impact on learning will be much greater if all of their peers are listening closely and thinking about whether they agree or disagree. Use move 7 regularly to achieve this: 'Junshik, what do you think of Rosemary's method?'

When pupils are commenting on characters' actions or feelings, use move 5 to probe for reasoning. Once your pupils get used to you asking this a lot, you won't need to because they will know you always expect evidence.

When you ask a question and a pupil gives a short response, instead of moving on, use move 2 to encourage them to elaborate. Often you'll find they go from a one-word response to several well-made points.

Teaching tip

As you start to ask for evidence, say: 'When I ask you "Why do you think that?" or "What's your evidence?" I'm not telling you you're wrong. It's that I really want to understand your thinking!'

Taking it further

See https://inquiryproject.terc.edu/index.html for information about how these teacher talk moves were used in a project about talk in science.

IDEA 57

P4C

P4C gives children a voice. *SENDCo*

Philosophy for Children (P4C) is a dialogic learning approach that enables children to discuss big ideas and challenging questions in a safe and structured way.

Teaching tip

For P4C to work, you will need to show your pupils that you are genuinely interested in their ideas and things that matter to them (see Idea 5). You will also need to work hard to put the essentials in place – for example, embedding respectful listening by all and an atmosphere of thinking together to gain understanding.

Taking it further

Look at the DialogueWorks and SAPERE websites for resources and inspiration. Search and sign up for accredited P4C training.

P4C was the brainchild of Matthew Lipman. With Ann Margaret Sharp, he wrote and pioneered a programme in the 1970s.

In P4C, pupils engage with a stimulus and ask big questions related to it. For example, they might read a story such as *The Little Red Hen* and wonder afterwards, 'Should we always help?'

There are two essential elements at the heart of P4C:
1. The 'Community of Enquiry' – your class create a place of mutual respect and attention-giving, combined with the search for understanding, meaning, truth and values supported by reasons.
2. The 4Cs: Caring thinking, Collaborative thinking, Creative thinking and Critical thinking.

When a class become practised at P4C, they embody positive talk and thinking behaviours. They listen carefully and try to understand each other. They give reasons and ask others for evidence. They spot assumptions. They support and challenge each other's points. They strive to see things from different perspectives.

P4C can be used across the curriculum to deepen thinking around core concepts. For example, pupils might ask 'Is invasion ever acceptable?' (history) or 'Should people try to stop erosion?' (geography).

IDEA 58

Tell *us*

It really enforces the idea that we're learning together. *Year 6 teacher*

Rather than the teacher saying 'Tell me', try saying 'Tell us' or 'Tell everyone'.

Have you noticed the following when you ask questions? The pupil responding looks only at you; they talk only to you, the teacher. Their classmates are passively waiting – they're not giving their attention to the pupil speaking. Why does this happen? Because the pupil speaking is not speaking *to them*.

This is very common in classrooms, and it's inadvertently encouraged by teacher talk such as: 'Can you say that again for *me*, please?', 'Who can tell *me* what might happen next?', 'Find *me* a phrase that describes how he is feeling.'

Try saying 'Tell us' or 'Tell everyone' instead.

This is one tiny tweak for teachers but a huge change for learners. You are now sending the message that pupil comments are for everyone's benefit. You are creating the conditions for others to consider the response, and to build on or challenge it. You are giving the rest of the class a reason to listen. You are helping to deliver the benefits of pupil-to-pupil dialogue.

Teaching tip

Try this every day for a few weeks until it becomes a habit. See if you can catch yourself saying 'Tell me' – and try to change it. You can even be transparent with the children: 'Actually, don't tell me – tell everyone!' See also Idea 3.

IDEA 59

Circles are worth it!

Working in a circle invites everybody to take part. Nobody shies away from talking. *Year 3 teacher*

Take time to sit in a circle on the carpet, or move back the tables to create a circle of chairs to improve communication.

Circles are brilliant for whole-class talk:
- Everyone can see each other easily.
- Voices travel better because there are no physical obstacles.
- Everyone can see who is speaking.
- Everyone can easily give attention to the speaker.
- You can do games and activities where everyone has a turn (see Idea 24).
- It's easy to use talking objects (see Idea 23).
- It's great for switching quickly between whole-class and talk partners (see Idea 44).
- It's easy for children to change partners quickly.

Create opportunities for your class to sit in a circle. With younger children, sitting on the carpet is a good, quick, easy option. With older children, it's worth moving furniture and making a circle of chairs. Once your class get used to doing this quickly and sensibly, it doesn't take long. Or, have some children help at playtime or lunchtime.

Make sure that the circle is a good circle:
- Everyone needs to be able to see each other; ensure no one is slightly in front or behind.
- No one should be squashed or uncomfortable.

Many talk games work particularly well in circles – for example, What would you do if... (Idea 75) or The imagination game (Idea 77).

Teaching tip

To help children project their voices and be audible, encourage them to direct their talk to the person opposite them in the circle.

Taking it further

If you're struggling to get your class to talk to each other instead of you, occasionally sit outside the circle for a few moments, and ask them to continue the discussion among themselves. (See also Idea 60.)

Bonus idea ★

Eye contact challenge: When you first set up the circle, do a quick eye contact activity. Say: 'Try to make eye contact with every single person in the circle. When you have, fold your arms.'

IDEA 60

Speaker chooses

Molly, I'd like to know what you think. *Age 8*

An engaging way to pass the dialogue over to your pupils — the last person to speak chooses the next person.

When you want to get pupil responses, instead of you deciding who speaks next, ask each speaker to choose the next one. Tell your class to use an agreed signal if they want to speak.

Encourage them to use questions, as well as the person's name: 'What do you think, Jacob?', 'Tanika, do you agree or disagree?'

This idea gets children to talk to each other, rather than always to the teacher. They start to look at each other more. They start to listen to each other more. It's transformational — they really start to solve things together as a whole class.

You can let children choose the next speaker for a few minutes here and there or throughout the day in different lessons. It doesn't have to take very long; it could be a chain of just two or three pupils speaking.

If you notice that the same pupils are often being chosen, address this. Say things like:
- 'I've noticed that only some of you are talking — what can we do to include everyone?'
- 'Choose someone who hasn't spoken yet.'

When you're planning, think carefully about moments where this sort of whole-class pupil-to-pupil dialogue could have a positive impact on learning. For example, predictions in science or English, or discussions about feelings and beliefs in PHSE.

> **Taking it further**
>
> Instead of pupils signalling that they want to speak, set an expectation that everyone should always be ready to contribute. Then, have each speaker choose anyone they want to hear from. They might choose someone who hasn't spoken yet: 'What are you thinking, Lily-Mae?'

> **Bonus idea** ★
>
> To keep your teacher talk concise and not interrupt the flow of learning, train your class to recognise that the short phrase 'Over to you' means 'you choose the next speaker'. Pair this with a teacher hand signal — eventually you won't need to say the phrase!

IDEA 61

Popcorn

It teaches us how to wait our turn and not speak over each other. If two people do, they just decide quickly between them who will speak. *Age 10*

Give your pupils opportunities to speak to the class without you organising whose turn it is.

Teaching tip
Be clear and transparent with your instructions, so pupils know at all times which 'participation system' for class discussion is being used.

Instead of always choosing who speaks, it's useful sometimes to let your class figure it out for themselves. Some people call this 'kind calling out' (Jane Considine) or 'talk into the space'.

A class that's used to Popcorn can quickly share thoughts and ideas. So, if you are working on synonyms for 'happy', at an appropriate moment you could say Popcorn and they will share multiple examples very quickly: 'joyful', 'content', 'buoyant', 'elated', 'delighted' and so on.

When you first introduce this to your class, say, 'When we do Popcorn, anyone can speak, but only one person at a time. I'm not going to decide who speaks or in what order.' Then it's over to them.

If they don't get it straight away, keep practising. They'll get used to it, and gain important oracy skills along the way. After all, in real-life situations there isn't usually someone organising the talk. Children need to have opportunities to learn how to get their voice heard.

Popcorn works well with one-word contributions, but also with longer comments. Here are two examples of when you might use it across the curriculum:
- 'How might Jacinda be feeling at this point in the story?'
- 'Yes, 17 is a prime number. Which other numbers below 100 are prime numbers?'

Bonus idea ★
Scribe while they are calling out ideas. They will see that you are listening and want their thoughts; this will make them more confident to speak.

IDEA 62

Stand up to speak up

I feel like the teacher! Age 7

Get pupils to stand to speak to the class — this helps their voice carry and will help everyone know who is speaking.

During whole-class talk when pupils are sitting at tables, say: 'Today I want you to stand up when it's your turn to speak. Just stand up where you are — you don't need to tuck your chair in.'

There are many benefits of having pupils stand sometimes when they talk to the class:

- Pupil talk gains status. It becomes a resource for learning.
- Everyone knows who's speaking! This sounds obvious, but often pupils are not sure where a voice is coming from in a busy classroom.
- The pupil will be much more audible due to their standing posture and fewer obstructions.
- It makes giving attention to the speaker easier. (See also Idea 38.)
- The speaker knows they are being listened to and that what they say is being valued in the learning.
- Being able to stand and speak confidently is a good life skill.

When pupils stand to speak it changes the classroom dynamic. Teachers often stand while talking to the class; having pupils stand equalises things a little. Enhance this further by sitting down sometimes during whole-class talk — so the pupil 'has the floor'. Place an extra chair at the side of the classroom so you have somewhere to sit (sitting at the side means you are less of a focal point).

Teaching tip

Standing up to speak can be used when one pupil summarises their group's discussion after exploratory talk (see Idea 50).

IDEA 63

They ramble on!

What about the kids who talk too much? *Year 5 teacher*

Sensitive and effective ways to help children be concise.

Teaching tip
Be the change you want to see. Don't ramble on yourself!

Taking it further
Model going off on a tangent, then create a new job: 'The Tangent Minder'. This person signals when someone starts to go off-topic.

Bonus idea ★
If you always interpret or clarify what a pupil has just said, they won't learn to make their point clearly. Instead, give opportunities for pupils to repeat or rephrase; ask them to 'Say it again, clearly'. With each attempt, clarity will improve.

One potential problem with whole-class dialogue is that some pupils take up a lot of airtime. This can cause others to disengage, and affects pace. We may worry that by interrupting, we'll damage someone's confidence. It can be tempting to avoid choosing children who 'ramble on'. But, as with 'quiet children', we must support them to develop their oracy skills, rather than ignore the problem.

First, check yourself — are they really 'rambling'? (See Idea 5.)

There are many reasons why children might talk excessively, so respond accordingly. For a pupil who has rarely spoken, consider just letting them talk. For a pupil with additional needs, make sure your approach fits your overall strategy for them.

When appropriate, don't be afraid to stop pupils. Here are some useful phrases:
- I'm going to stop you there. Tell us what your main idea is in one sentence.
- How does that fit with the question?
- Are you saying...? (See Idea 56)
- We'll come back to that at another time. I'll make a note.
- I'll discuss that with you in a moment.
- Could you explain that to Miss H?

Give responsibilities and challenges, as appropriate: 'Florence, I'm going to ask you to summarise — take notes please', 'Ewan, your job is to ask for clarification if someone isn't making their point clearly', 'Phan, jot down the key words — I'll ask you to tell us six at the end.'

Talk for different purposes

Part 7

IDEA 64

The art of argument

Raise your words, not your voice. *Rumi, ancient poet*

Create opportunities for pupils to learn and practise the key skills of argument.

Taking it further
Set up whole-class debates. Search online for 'debating resources for primary schools'.

Example statements to debate:

- The school day should be shorter.
- We should be able to choose which lessons we do.
- All schools should grow vegetables.
- History is more important than geography.
- Children should be able to use mobile phones in school.

Set this up in in pairs or fours. Pupils take sides – arguing in favour or against the statement, using the prompts. They tick when they use them, or an observer ticks. Pupils swap sides after a period of time.

- ☐ Ask for evidence: 'How do you know?'
- ☐ Use examples: 'An example is...'
- ☐ Explain from a different perspective: 'Let's look at this from a different angle...'
- ☐ Connect to their values: 'I know you believe...'
- ☐ Refer back to key points: 'As I said earlier...'
- ☐ Speak in lists: 'I have three main points...'
- ☐ Use 'I': 'I feel that it's better if...'
- ☐ Understand before you respond: 'Please could you clarify...'
- ☐ Present another argument: 'Also I'd like to add...'
- ☐ Disagree with a point: 'I disagree because...'
- ☐ Appeal to common sense: 'There is no doubt that...'
- ☐ Show your feelings: 'I'm worried that...'
- ☐ Be polite! 'You've made a good point but...'
- ☐ State your reasons: 'The reason I think...'
- ☐ Keep it focused: 'We're getting off topic...'

Bonus idea ★
Search online for the 'Good Reasoning Tree' from Will Ord.

IDEA 65

Common ground

Negotiation is to try to find a place where you both agree. *Age 9*

Oracy challenges to practise using the language of negotiation and consensus-building.

Set up scenarios that pose an interesting problem for pupils to solve. Create role cards for three imaginary children with contrasting views.

Example scenario
Pupils choose a fourth classroom rule for an imaginary class that already has three rules: Be respectful. Be organised. Be hard-working. Pupils work in trios, each taking one of the following role cards. They take turns to explain their proposed rule, then negotiate until they agree on what the new rule should be.

> **Groupy Grayson** enjoys groupwork and wants everyone to have opportunities to contribute and be heard. – 'Let's have a rule to take turns during group discussions!'

> **Personal Polly** enjoys collaborating but also needs time for independent thinking. – 'Let's have a rule to not interrupt when someone is working independently!'

> **Happy Halima** enjoys helping classmates and boosting their spirits. – 'Let's have a rule that encourages kindness and positive words!'

Helpful negotiation phrases
'I hear what you're saying, and I agree with some parts, but...'
'Let's make sure everyone has a turn.'
'Let's try to include everyone's ideas.'
'Can we compromise and...'
'That's a great point, and we can also consider...'
'Let's discuss the pros and cons of each option.'
'I'm willing to give up this part if we can include...'

> **Teaching tip**
>
> Give opportunities for everyone to practise saying the negotiation phrases first – call and repeat.

> **Bonus idea** ★
>
> Try this as a 'fishbowl' activity, with three children in the centre of the circle and the rest of the class listening with a tick list of the negotiation phrases.

IDEA 66

Public speaking takes practice!

I'm kind of shy, but ever since we've been practising the skills of voice projection and expression I've started to gain confidence and can now stand up and talk in front of everyone. Age 8

Public speaking, or presentational talk, is one aspect of oracy. It's a good skill to develop because it's clearly useful in various life and work situations. We know many adults are nervous of speaking in public; if we teach it and give numerous opportunities to practise, we might see a new generation of confident public speakers.

Teaching tip

Be careful not to set your pupils up to fail by asking them to do presentational talk on something that they don't know much about. They will need time to research, plan and possibly discuss with peers. Be mindful that presentational talk is different from exploratory talk and partial thinking (see Ideas 50 and 4).

Taking it further

Enable pupils to record themselves practising their presentations on video or audio. They could self-assess and compare to role models in example speeches.

Using the Oracy Skills Framework, a good public speaker:

Physical
- speaks loudly and clearly enough
- does not speak too quickly, pauses purposefully and looks their audience in the eye
- varies their tone to engage the audience
- looks comfortable (no pacing or fiddling)
- has confident posture and body language
- uses gestures to emphasise and engage

Linguistic
- uses an appropriate style of language
- uses humour, repetition and rhetorical questions to engage their audience
- uses phrases appropriate to the context, e.g. 'Thank you for your attention', 'We are here today to talk about...', 'No one can deny that...'
- uses specific and precise vocabulary

Cognitive
- chooses appropriate content and presents it in a coherent order, linking ideas together
- plans and delivers their presentation in the allotted time; summarises effectively

- convinces their audience through justifications, including evidence and examples

Social and emotional
- manages their emotions to appear confident
- is aware of their audience – their prior knowledge, opinions, mood and so on
- shows enthusiasm for their subject.

What is public speaking?
Help your class to compile a list of all the times when public speaking is used – for example, announcements in public places, assemblies, political or persuasive speeches, welcoming people to an event, weddings, funerals, parties, sports events, sales pitches, organising and delegating in an emergency, and so on.

Practise
A good way to get pupils to begin practising public speaking is to start small. Trios work well – taking turns to speak to each other and giving useful feedback (see Idea 8), building up to presenting to the whole class.

Provide different audiences – for example, younger classes, headteacher, assembly or parents.

There are other occasions when pupils can gain purposeful public speaking practice in school:

- giving announcements to other classes
- recording a message for the school answerphone
- greeting visitors
- opening and closing remarks in assemblies
- summaries after group talk tasks
- announcements during school events such as summer fair, sports day and so on
- curriculum presentations (see Idea 96).

Make sure you also give frequent opportunities for pupils to come up to the front of the class to read out their work, explain how they worked out a maths problem, and so on.

> **Teaching tip**
>
> Show video and audio examples of public speaking. For example, it's easy to find powerful political and persuasive speeches online; search for 'great speeches' or 'great speeches by young people'. Ask pupils what they notice, and what they like or don't like. Challenge them to spot different techniques such as humour, gesture, metaphor, tone, repetition, summary and so on.

> **Bonus idea** ★
>
> Non-verbal 'follow the leader' games can get children used to being the centre of attention. Choose a child to be the leader. Ask them to do a simple action. Everyone else needs to look at the leader and copy the action that they are doing. Choose the next leader and repeat.

IDEA 67

Tell us a story!

I like it when my teacher tells us a story. I can see what she's saying. It goes in. *Age 10*

Storytelling — different to reading — is an all-embracing way to enable children to develop the physical, linguistic, cognitive and social and emotional skills of oracy, because it requires combining these aspects in a unified way.

> **Teaching tip**
>
> Before telling a story, prepare your opening sentences and ending, so that you can begin and end confidently.

The more stories you tell, the better listeners your pupils will become. The more stories *they* tell, the better talkers they will become.

Activities to exercise the storytelling muscles

Babble gabble: After a story, pairs sit facing each other and retell it together as quickly as possible, hardly pausing for thought, within a set time limit of 90 seconds. Repeat with different partners. Consider deliberately pairing up 'quiet children' for this, so they have good opportunities to speak.

Fortunately… unfortunately: One player begins the story with a problem. For example, 'Once there was a tiger who was trapped by a magic spell in the body of a mouse…' The next player continues, beginning 'Fortunately…', then the next continues with, 'Unfortunately…' – and so the story is built up. This game works well in trios, after it's been modelled.

Finish it: Tell a short story, but stop just before the end. Ask pairs to invent an ending. Then repeat your final sentence and invite children to continue seamlessly with their versions to the whole class.

Seven images: In pairs or trios, children condense a story into seven key images. This promotes visualisation and memory, and creates prompts to retell the story. (Most short traditional tales can be reduced in this way.)

> **Bonus idea** ★
>
> As a school, aim for every teacher and teaching assistant to learn and practise one story that they can tell in different moments to different groups of children. It's a fabulous thing for everyone to have up their sleeve for those moments of suddenly covering a class for ten minutes.

IDEA 68

Talking to build friendships

I've now got ways to make new friends in high school. *Age 11.*

Help children practise the skills of 'small talk' to build relationships.

1. Cut up the sentences below and have pupils sort them into questions, comments and compliments.
2. Ask pupils to imagine there is a new child in their class, or that they are standing in the dinner line next to someone they don't really know. Tell them to pick a few phrases that they might say in these situations. Role play this.
3. Ask them to reflect in pairs or as a class which they prefer giving or receiving: questions, comments or compliments?
4. In pairs, ask them to invent a few more questions, comments and compliments, and to practise role playing them.

> **Teaching tip**
>
> Make pupils aware of the importance of genuine (rather than fake) compliments. Support and challenge them to practise giving compliments about things beyond appearance.

Questions
'What did you think of that maths lesson?'
'Where do you live?'
'Are you feeling better today?'
'Why were you off school yesterday?'
Comments
'Nice and sunny today!'
'This apple pie is delicious!'
'That writing was really difficult!'
'Sports Day was fun!'
Compliments
'I like your scarf.'
'That was so nice that you helped Jonas.'
'You were really patient when Sally was messing about earlier!'
'You've got really neat handwriting!'

Some neurodivergent pupils, and pupils with social anxiety, sometimes find it hard to start conversations. These phrases provide useful openers. Create opportunities to practise throughout the year.

> **Bonus idea** ★
>
> Compliment lines: Divide the class into two rows facing each other so everyone has a partner. Children take turns with their partner to give each other a compliment. Then a child at one end moves to the other end, and everyone from that row steps sideways to their next partner. The compliments continue!

IDEA 69

Experimenting with ways of speaking

I had to speak very politely when my Granny was around – she likes manners very much! Age 7

A fun activity to raise awareness of how people sometimes adjust the way they speak.

Changing how we speak in different situations is common, and can be a useful skill. However, this is a complex area of oracy:

- There's no single correct way to talk.
- Adjusting your speaking style for your audience and situation can demonstrate empathy and help people listen to you.
- Sometimes people feel pressured to change how they speak to fit in.

Start to raise awareness of this by asking, 'Have you ever changed the way you speak because of the situation you are in?' Pupils might mention speaking more slowly when talking to a friend who is learning English, or using different words with different people such as parents and friends.

Activity

Model how this might look in a local shop:
More formal: 'Good morning, madam. I would very much like to purchase some of your finest chocolate. Thank you, that's awfully kind of you.'
Less formal: 'Hiya mate. Give us one of them, will ya? 75p, yeh? Cheers. Nice one. Later.'
Challenge your pupils to try out different 'registers' in the following situations. Tell them to start informal and gradually make it more formal. How formal can they go?

- Somebody's standing in your way.
- Persuade someone to lend you £1,000.
- You're phoning to complain about a big bill.

Teaching tip

Be open minded and inclusive with regard to different accents and dialects. The critical thing is that children know how to communicate effectively with others in a wide range of situations.

Taking it further

After doing this activity, ask your class a reflection question: 'Of the phrases you tried out, which would be the most appropriate?'

Bonus idea ★

Check out the British Library Sound Archives – a treasure trove, including hundreds of recordings of diverse accents and dialects.

Talk games

Part 8

IDEA 70

Find someone who...

You get better at learning while you're talking! *Age 8*

An active way to review learning across the curriculum.

Teaching tip

Use this idea to get pupils talking about learning at any point. It will help them remember recent learning, and give them an opportunity to apply vocabulary.

Create 'Find someone who' challenges related to recent learning. Everyone walks around, talking to different people. They need to get a different name against each statement, plus a brief note of what that person said.

Here's an example of reviewing last week's learning:

Find someone who...
- ☐ remembers how to start a formula in an Excel spreadsheet
- ☐ can tell you which character they most empathise with in our class novel
- ☐ can explain what a fair test is
- ☐ would rather live at a high altitude and can say why
- ☐ can explain what alliteration is

Here's another example, reviewing learning about the Vikings:

Find someone who...
- ☐ can tell you something interesting about the Vikings
- ☐ can tell you three facts about Viking ships
- ☐ can tell you what the Vikings did in England
- ☐ can tell you something they are wondering about the Vikings
- ☐ can tell you three things about Viking beliefs
- ☐ can explain to you where the Vikings travelled to

Bonus idea ★

Use this after the holidays to get everyone talking and finding out what others have been doing.

IDEA 71

Would you rather?

It's fun because you can keep swapping sides. If your friend is on the other side, they can convince you! *Age 7*

Inspired by John Burningham's fabulous book, these questions help children get better at explaining their thinking, convincing others and justifying opinions.

Give pupils a question starting with *Would you rather*, with two or more optional answers. Tell them they have to choose just one of the options and give a reason for their choice.

For example:
- Would you rather be friends with a pirate or a parrot?
- Would you rather make one person very happy, or make ten people a little bit happy?
- Would you rather collect sticks, conkers or autumn leaves?

Use *Would you rather* questions across the curriculum to promote thinking and talking:
- Would you rather be friends with the Gruffalo or the mouse?
- Would you rather meet Oliver Twist or the Artful Dodger?
- Would you rather be a Viking or an Anglo-Saxon?
- Would you rather discover a new species or save a species from going extinct?
- Would you rather use pastels, charcoal or watercolours?
- Would you rather hum the melody or sing the chorus?

Make sure that all options are equally legitimate; don't give an option that you wouldn't want them to pick! For example, as teachers we should be promoting regular exercise, so **don't** ask, 'Would you rather exercise every day or never exercise?'

Teaching tip

As always, remember that modelling and thinking time will help pupils respond successfully. To get them into the habit of always giving reasons, initially prompt with 'Why?'

Taking it further

Vary the wording sometimes: 'Which do you prefer...?', 'Which is more important...?' and so on.

Bonus idea ★

Make it dynamic by getting pupils to move something. For example, get them to show their choice by placing a counter in one of two pots. Or display the options on different sides of the room and tell pupils to move themselves to show their choice.

IDEA 72

Good idea/bad idea?

In history we tried 'Join the Roman army – good idea/bad idea?' Children used talk prompts to justify their reasons and respectfully challenge others. What amazed me was the level of engagement and thoughtful contributions from some of our lower-attaining pupils.
Year 3 teacher

This is such an effective talk structure. Present an idea and ask pupils if they think it is a good idea or a bad idea, and their reasons.

Teaching tip
For more question ideas, search online for 'Topsy Page thinking questions'.

Taking it further
Provide talk prompts (see Idea 18).

The key is to make sure there isn't one single correct answer; this means that many more pupils will speak up (see Idea 16).

Good idea/bad idea is easy to replicate. It promotes critical and creative thinking and allows pupils to see others' perspectives. Use it for quick, fun games or across the curriculum to develop learning through talk.

Example questions
- Talking sheep – good idea/bad idea?
- Extreme sports – good idea/bad idea?
- Robots – good idea/bad idea?
- Taking things from a beach – good idea/bad idea?
- Wandering through a forest – good idea/bad idea? (English – Goldilocks)
- Eating only seasonal fruit and veg – good idea/bad idea? (DT – cooking)
- Mining for resources – good idea/bad idea? (geography)
- Always using column subtraction – good idea/bad idea? (maths)

Example conversation
Talking sheep – good idea/bad idea?
James: I think if sheep could talk, it'd be fun.
Carlo: I'm not sure. They might say they're sad because people eat them.
Amina: They might not know that. We'd find out what they do know!

IDEA 73

Odd one out

The children's logical justifications were incredible! *Year 4 teacher*

An effective game for motivating everyone to talk, applying new vocabulary in context, valuing everyone's thoughts and ideas and developing reasoning and creative thinking.

- The idea of this game is that there is not one single, correct answer — there may be multiple possible answers (see Idea 16).
- Select three things. They could be objects, images, numbers, paragraphs, shapes and so on. Physical objects work well if you're sitting in a circle.
- Ask the class to think about which is the odd one out and why. (The other two objects must have something in common.)
- Children explain their ideas and justify them with reasons.
- Embrace their different perspectives. Encourage them to listen to each other and discuss differences of opinion.
- If children are struggling to identify an odd one out, prompt them first to find connections between two of the items.

Odd one out can be used across the curriculum. Here is an example from a reading lesson. You can see the thinking and the language of dialogue:

Tom: 'I think Fagin is the odd one out because he is an adult and the other two are children.'

Feiona: 'I think Oliver is the odd one out because he is innocent.'

Andres: 'I disagree because I believe all children are innocent, so the Artful Dodger must also be innocent.'

Teaching tip

Be careful not to create an odd one out with one correct answer that you are looking for. This will lose most of the benefits. The game works well if any of the options could be the odd one out for different reasons.

Taking it further

Display talk prompts alongside the objects, to support the dialogue (see Idea 18).

Bonus idea ★

Have three children each choose an object from around the classroom to use in odd one out. To extend the game, select a further child to swap one of the objects for a new one.

IDEA 74

Four corners

Children engage with their peers – spontaneously questioning and arguing. Also a fantastic diagnostic tool. *Headteacher*

Pupils move to the corner of the room to indicate which statement they agree with. As well as being a mechanism for productive dialogue, four corners provides an opportunity for you to hear what relevant vocabulary pupils use and what connections they are making to prior learning.

Display four options, each in a different corner of the room. Pupils look at all the options. They think, discuss with others, and stand in the corner they most agree with. If they're unsure, they stand in the middle to listen and think more.

Ask some pupils to explain why they chose their corner. Everyone listens and reflects. If anyone is persuaded by someone else's reasons, they can move. If someone moves, it's a great moment to ask them to explain their reasoning. Praise pupils for careful listening and thoughtful re-evaluation.

Examples
Storybook characters: Who would you most like to go on an adventure with? Goldilocks, Gretel, Cinderella, Little Red Riding Hood (display images).
Story openers: Read the four adventure story openers – which is the best? (Include strong elements in all four options, to raise the challenge and generate useful dialogue.)
Seeds: Which sentence do you agree with? 1. Seeds grow best in the dark. 2. Seeds are empty until they start to grow. 3. Seeds have to be in soil to grow. 4. Seeds need some food.
Explorers: Display the talking point 'Explorers are crazy!' Display in the four corners strongly agree/agree/disagree/strongly disagree.
Punctuation: Use identical wording in each of the four corners, but vary the punctuation. Ask pupils, 'Which option has the best punctuation?'

> **Teaching tip**
>
> Design your tasks to be 'low floor, high ceiling' to make the task more inclusive and allow children to talk at different depths.

IDEA 75

What would you do if...?

If I had a magic wand I would turn someone into a frog!
If I had a magic wand I would make a unicorn.
If I had a magic wand I would use it for kindness. *Age 5*

Pupils imagine themselves with new powers or in a new role. What would they do?

This is such a simple game but develops speaking and listening as well as critical and creative thinking. It can also give you an insight into your pupils' thoughts, concerns and ideas.

Ask your class a question that involves them imagining themselves in another role – for example, 'What would you do if you were the headteacher?' Pupils then take it in turns to say what they'd do.

This can be used as a standalone talk and thinking game. For example:
- If I were the king I would...
- If I were the prime minister I would...
- If I were in charge of the world I would...
- If I had super strength I would...
- If I could go anywhere I would...

It can also be used across the curriculum for pupils to apply new facts and vocabulary:
- If I were a predator I would...
- If I were a Tudor I would...
- If I were a mountaineer I would...
- If I were a tourist I would...

Teaching tip

This game works well when done as a round in a circle (see Idea 24).

Bonus idea ★

Pass a 'talking toy' around the circle to invite everyone to have a go – this could be a relevant prop such as a pretend magic wand or a crown, or a simple talking stone (see Idea 23).

IDEA 76

The beanbag game

The eye contact between the children was lovely to see. And it was really good to hear clear voices! Year 3 teacher

A fun game to develop eye contact, voice projection and more!

Teaching tip

After playing the game, ask the class to reflect: What skills is this game helping us practise or develop?

Taking it further

Here are three other variations: 'Let's do it now without speaking!', 'Let's see if we can do it in reverse order.', 'Let's time how long it takes to throw the beanbag to everyone – then we'll see whether we can get faster.'

- Stand with pupils in a circle.
- Tell everyone, 'There are two rules for the game. One: always throw to the same person. Two: say their name loudly and clearly before you throw.'
- Pick someone opposite you. Say their name loudly and clearly and throw the beanbag to them.
- They then say someone else's name, and throw to them.
- The beanbag is thrown across the circle until everyone has had one go.
- The last person throws it back to you.
- Continue, repeating the same sequence (see rule one).

More beanbags...

Introduce a second and third beanbag. This often creates a buzz of excitement! If needed, pause and ask if anyone has a tip for the group. Pupils will often suggest things like:

- 'Remember rule two – say the name before you throw! Make sure everyone can hear!'
- 'Look at the person who is throwing to you.'
- 'Don't rush – wait until you know they are ready.'

The beanbag game is useful for developing oracy skills including eye contact, turn-taking, voice projection and getting everyone used to speaking in a large group. It also develops collaboration and concentration.

IDEA 77

The imagination game

This game can help you speak better English and use better language! You might hear words you've never heard and then you might get to use them! *Age 8, multilingual learner*

The imagination game develops turn-taking, listening, responding, talking to an audience and creative thinking. Pupils pass a simple-shaped object around the circle, say what else it could be, and do an action.

Teacher: This is a plastic plate and it is also a giant full stop! [Holds plate up in front.]

Bryce: This is a giant full stop and it is also my special hat! [Places plate on head.]

Linh: This is my special hat and it is also the moon in the sky! [Holds plate up high.] ...etc.

The key phrase 'and it is also' enables children to practise building on someone else's idea. Orally rehearse this before starting.

What if a child repeats an idea? This depends on the child. Sometimes repeating represents success, for example if they're new to English or if this is the first time they've had the courage to speak to the class. For others, it may be appropriate to challenge them to think of a new idea.

What if some children don't have any ideas? One option is to ask children to signal when they have an idea (for example, by folding arms) and passing the object to the next person showing the signal. Continue going round in this manner – gradually everyone will join in.

What if the child's idea isn't relevant to the object? Be careful – children's creative ideas can be 'correct' in ways you don't immediately recognise! If you can't see any connection, ask them to explain or justify.

Teaching tip

Play the game as a whole class or in small groups. Objects you could use include a cardboard tube, a bottle top, a cube, string or a stick. Pupils only need to repeat the idea from the person just before them – they don't need to remember everyone's!

IDEA 78

Word connect

The more thinking skills, the more faster you'll get the words out!
Age 8

This a great game to develop listening. It also improves key thinking skills such as connecting ideas and justifying with reasons.

Teaching tip

When you first play Word connect, ask pupils to include reasons. This helps everyone to understand the game, and develops reasoning. For example: 'Pen, because we use pens to write on paper.'

Taking it further

When pupils are confident at Word connect, time them to see how long it takes the whole class to each say a connecting word, and then see whether they can beat their time. This will help them practise quick thinking!

This fun game works well as a whole-class game in a circle or in small groups. The idea is to listen to the word said by the person before you, and then say a word that has a connection.
For example, start with the word 'table'. The first pupil needs to think of a word that has a connection to 'table'. Then the game continues around the class: 'Paper' – 'Pen' – 'Plastic' – 'Toy' – 'Shop' ... and so on.

Word disconnect

Once your class are used to making connections, try this version. It will help them develop respectful challenge and reasoning.

Say a word – for example, 'tree'. Pupils try to think of a word that has no connection.
Teacher: Hmmm. Let's all have a think. Which words have no connection with 'tree'?
Ryan: Lolly!
Haroon (after thinking time): I disagree. Ice lollies have wooden sticks made from trees!
Teacher: Good connection, Haroon. OK, let's think again. Are there any words that have absolutely no connection with 'tree'?

Continue until a word is suggested for which no one can think of a challenge. For example:
Tahlia: Carpet.
Teacher (after a long pause): No challenges! So, now let's try to think of a word with no connection to 'carpet'.
Henry (after thinking time): Garden!
Lena: I respectfully challenge – my grandad uses old carpet in his garden to stop the weeds!

IDEA 79

Ten-word challenge

It makes children more thoughtful. It makes them stop and think before they talk. *Year 3 teacher*

A collaborative talk game — less is more!

Tell pupils to take turns with a partner to create a ten-word story. For example:

'We're going to do a ten-word story challenge starting with an animal. Partner A — start by choosing an animal. Partner B — follow it with a verb. Then continue taking turns until you have a ten-word story that makes sense. Make sure one of you is counting on your fingers so you can both see how many words you've used. If it doesn't make sense, stop and start again.'
The story might go something like this:
Fox... decided... to... explore... her... new... forest... and... found... Dog!

This game helps pupils develop skills including listening closely, turn-taking and collaborative thinking. It also helps them make thoughtful word choices.
Ten-word challenge can be used to work on statements, explanations or definitions across the curriculum. For example:

- Can you explain what 'food chain' means in exactly ten words?
- Can you give your prediction in exactly ten words?
- Can you summarise the paragraph about Ancient Egyptian pyramids in exactly ten words?

Variation: think first, then talk
Pupils work independently to come up with a ten-word sentence about the current topic. They compare sentences with a partner, and then share them verbally with the whole class. Use random selection (Idea 20) or a round (Idea 24).

Teaching tip

As with all pair talk tasks, it's much more likely that pupils will succeed if you model first. Modelling can be done with a colleague or with a pupil. If asking pupils to help you model, make sure you vary who you choose; this is a useful oracy development opportunity and shouldn't be limited to the same few pupils.

Taking it further

Once your class have got used to Ten-word challenge, you can set different word limits. This will challenge them to vary sentence structure.

IDEA 80

Give one, get one

I like it because it gives people ideas of what you think. Age 9

Pupils walk around the space to swap ideas. This interactive activity works well when you want everyone to remember learning, or when you want pupils to generate new ideas. It's an alternative to asking recall questions or seeking volunteers with ideas. It ensures that everyone in the room has plenty of material to work with, even if they start with nothing or very little.

Teaching tip

Remind children to give and get just one. That way they will have multiple short interactions with many different classmates.

For example, to recap the work you've been doing on wild mammals in Britain:

1. Ask pupils to write at least one mammal on their paper or whiteboard. Some pupils may write several.
2. After everyone has written at least one, ask them to stand up.
3. Tell them to talk to someone else and to give this person one mammal from their list. They also need to get a new mammal from them.
4. As soon as they have done this, they move to a new person.
5. When you stop them, they should all have a good number of mammals on their paper.

Give one, get one across the curriculum:
- weather phrases to create mood at the start of an adventure story (English)
- range of emotions (PHSE)
- facts about Ancient Egyptians (history)
- positives of globalisation (geography).

Further benefits of Give one, get one
- It develops children's social and emotional oracy skills as they talk to different people. They might start by approaching friends, but then realise that others have different ideas.
- It often requires children to explain, question and clarify. This develops collaborative thinking.
- The talk element makes the learning much more memorable and enjoyable.

IDEA 81

Yes, and...

It's a great game to help them understand the idea of building on other people's ideas. *Year 3 teacher*

You can use this fun game in oracy lessons to get everyone talking. It increases confidence and develops the skills of listening, building and making connections, reasoning and responding. It's also fantastic to use across the curriculum to consolidate learning and apply vocabulary.

Yes, and... is often played in pairs. One person starts with a 'lead-in' phrase, then every turn starts with 'Yes, and...'

Here's an example:
'At playtime, let's do some skipping.'
'**Yes, and** let's try saying that rhyme we learned.'
'**Yes, and** we can invite some friends to join in.'
'**Yes, and** after that let's rest in the sun.'
... And so on.

Try it for remembering stories. Here's an example of children retelling *Some Dogs Do* by Jez Alborough:
'At the beginning, Sid was happy.'
'**Yes, and** he could fly in the sky!'
'**Yes, and** he told his friends he could fly.'
'**Yes, and** they were mean to him.'
'**Yes, and** he tried to convince them that he really could fly.'
'**Yes, and** he fell on the floor.'
'**Yes, and** he felt very sad.'
... And so on.

Try it in other lessons to help children remember what they have learned:
'The Ancient Maya worshipped many gods.'
'**Yes, and** goddesses.'
'**Yes, and** they liked building cities.'
'**Yes, and** they grew maize.'
... And so on.

Taking it further

Some children will also benefit from practising 'Yes, but...' to help them develop confidence to disagree: 'Let's go back in time to the Stone Age!', 'Yes, but then I'll have no phone!', 'Yes, but you'll have lots of time to explore and play!', 'Yes, but I might have to catch an animal to eat!', 'Yes, but it will be interesting using flint tools!'

IDEA 82

Opinion continuums

It was exciting to hear different people's ideas! *Age 6*

Promote discussion and encourage reflection by having pupils stand along a line to show their opinion.

Keep a long rope or ribbon handy in your oracy tray. Place it on the floor with big labels at each end. Pupils then position themselves along the line, depending on their opinion. The idea is to hear different ideas, thoughts and reasons.

Here are two ways you can organise continuums, with some examples:

Option 1: One statement – agree/disagree

- Public speaking is exciting.
- Listening is more important than speaking.
- Mobile phones are good for children.

◄─────────────────────────────►
AGREE   Public speaking is exciting   DISAGREE

Option 2: Two contrasting statements

- Healthy eating is boring/Healthy eating is exciting
- Animals make great pets/Animals shouldn't be pets
- School uniforms are beneficial/School uniforms are unnecessary

◄─────────────────────────────►
Healthy eating is boring   Healthy eating is exciting

For continuums to be successful, it's essential that you create a supportive and non-judgemental environment, where each child's experience and perspective is respected and valued (see Part 1).

Teaching tip

Take care when designing these activities to make sure there are definitely multiple valid opinions. Don't unthinkingly create an activity in which children can be 'wrong' – in terms of laws, school rules or values. For example, **don't** ask 'Bullying is bad – agree/disagree?'

Taking it further

Fold the line: Once pupils are on the continuum, get them to move so that the line is effectively folded in half and pupils are facing each other. Those with the most opposite views will be facing each other in pairs. Ask them to take turns explaining and justifying their opinions.

IDEA 83

Bring it to life!

When you talk, you don't just use words – you use your hands and feelings to connect with people and make them feel what you're feeling. *Age 9*

When your class are using storytelling or anecdotes to entertain, persuade, or give information, challenge them to use different aspects of physical oracy to bring their words to life.

Physical oracy techniques
- [ ] a hand gesture to emphasise a point
- [ ] a happy facial expression
- [ ] a sad facial expression
- [ ] a shocked facial expression
- [ ] a serious facial expression
- [ ] a surprised facial expression
- [ ] a loud voice for an exciting moment
- [ ] a quiet voice for a mysterious moment
- [ ] a jolly voice for a funny or happy section
- [ ] a pause to create suspense
- [ ] eye contact with the audience

Provide opportunities for pupils to practise speaking in pairs or trios with the above tick list. For example, one pupil retells a story while the other two tick off the techniques that they notice. (For younger pupils, choose just three target techniques and make a tick sheet with visual symbols.)

Variations
Ask pupils to spot physical oracy techniques when you tell a story. Pause and ask, 'Which have you spotted so far?' Or, as you tell the story, pupils indicate every time they notice a technique by putting their thumbs up.
Or you could simply ask them to copy you when you do a technique. For example, when you do a surprised expression, they all copy it. 'Show me your surprised faces!'

> **Teaching tip**
>
> To ensure that pupils understand these physical oracy techniques and get better at them over time, do frequent storytelling yourself using them. Also, give them opportunities to hear – and see – other people tell stories in an animated way. For example, visitors, librarians or online story videos (ensure they are quality examples – try Storytime on the BookTrust YouTube channel).

> **Taking it further**
>
> After your class have practised and developed physical oracy techniques, challenge them to do a one-minute speech, or retell an event or story, without using any at all! Prohibit hand movements and allow only a neutral face. They will suddenly realise how important these physical aspects of oracy are!

IDEA 84

PMIQ

If you do PMIQ you can find out what other people think. Age 6

To develop productive talk in your classroom, try providing simple structures to encourage pupils to think more deeply and express their thoughts. PMIQ, based on an idea from Edward de Bono, is a wonderful, simple to use structure.

Teaching tip

As always, use strategies to manage the talk and make sure that everyone gets a chance to join in.

Taking it further

Search online for 'de Bono thinking lessons'.

In PMIQ, pupils discuss a task or idea using four headings:

P plus (positive)
M minus (challenge)
I interesting
Q question

PMIQ can be used across the curriculum:
- to reflect on an activity
- to discuss a single talking point
- to think things through
- to help make decisions.

Example 1: Pupils reflecting on making a pulley to raise the sail on their Viking ship.
P 'It was really fun seeing the sail go up when we pulled the string.'
M 'It was difficult to get the mast to stick to the deck.'
I 'It was interesting to learn how a pulley could be made from cardboard circles.'
Q 'How could we make our mast stronger?'

Example 2: Discussing the talking point 'Every school should have a pet dog.'
P 'Stroking dogs makes you feel calm.'
M 'Some people are scared of dogs.'
I 'At some schools, children read to the dog!'
Q 'Who will look after the dog at night?'

Used regularly, structures like this will become familiar and easy to apply. They can be used in pair talk, group talk and whole-class talk.

IDEA 85

Don't forget barrier games!

It's a challenge. You have to really try to understand what they are talking about and listen really carefully! When you talk you have to be really precise and make it as simple as possible. *Age 9*

Barrier games promote active listening, clear communication and the ability to give and follow instructions. They also encourage turn-taking, collaboration and problem-solving.

Two pupils are separated by a barrier (such as a propped-up mini whiteboard) and must communicate effectively to complete a task. They can do this through verbal descriptions, asking questions and seeking clarification. (They can't point or show.)

Build a structure: Give each child an identical set of approximately ten toy bricks. Place a barrier between them and instruct one child to invent a simple structure using their bricks. The other child must listen carefully to their partner's instructions and try to replicate the structure using their own bricks.

Drawing challenge: Provide one child with paper and pens. Place a barrier between them. Give the other child a picture that their partner cannot see. The child with the picture describes it in detail to their partner, who tries to draw it based solely on the verbal description. Pupils compare the drawings to see how well they communicated.

Map exploration: Give each child a copy of a simple map with landmarks and pathways, plus a counter. Place a barrier between them. One child is the 'guide' and must provide clear directions to help their partner navigate the map to reach various destinations. They move their counters as they go.

Teaching tip

Encourage pupils to ask clarifying questions. Model this.

Taking it further

Try a barrier game with one-way communication – only the child explaining is allowed to speak! After a few minutes, ask the silent pupils how they felt. Repeat the game, but this time the listener can ask their partner to repeat, clarify, slow down and so on, as normal. This highlights the importance of two-way communication and feedback.

Part 9

Embedding oracy

IDEA 86

Infuse your curriculum with oracy

It really helps me when we get to talk in lessons. Age 10

Build learning through talk into your planning. Here are some examples of planned questions or activities for meaningful learning through talk across the different curriculum subjects. There are more examples and details throughout this book.

Teaching tip

In different subjects, when presenting pupils with a task or problem, organise some structured talk before they start: 'Have a think about how we could solve this. Before picking up your pencil, pass the talking cube around your group of three, and listen to each other's ideas.'

Art and design
- Which shading technique does your partner prefer – hatching or stippling? Why?

Computing
- Instructor/operator pair challenge. For example, the instructor has traffic data on paper and the operator has control of the computer. The instructor explains to the operator how to set out the spreadsheet and what data to input. The operator is not allowed to look at the paper but is allowed to ask clarifying questions.

Design and technology
- With your partner, order the cut-up statements from least important to most important criteria for designing a mini-greenhouse (see Idea 30).

English
- Pupils retell a story in groups of three, taking turns to pass a talking toy.

Geography
- Walk around the classroom and look at the images on the tables. Which ones do you think are of India and which aren't? What are your justifications? Discuss with others.

History
- Is the seaside more fun now than it was in the past?

Languages
- Use target language talk prompts in rounds, such as 'Hoy me siento…'
- Use cut-ups (Idea 30) – for example, 'With your partner match each phrase to the correct situation.'
- Try Give one, get one (Idea 80) – for example, colours.

Maths
- We've tried two different methods. In pairs, discuss which method you prefer and why.

Music
- How did that piece of music make you feel? Which instruments could you hear? Take turns to discuss with your partner. Try to use some of our key words. Display vocabulary: tempo, pitch, dynamics, etc.
- Explain to your partner the three things we need to remember when we're working on our xylophone technique. (After playing: Now tell your partner what they did well and what they can improve.)

Physical education
- Is it OK to take risks to win?
- Peer feedback using target words and phrases (prepare vocabulary cards to take outside, if you have time).

PSHE
- Use Popcorn (Idea 61) to list ways of looking after our mental health.

Religious education
- Sort the beliefs and practices cut-up cards into Buddhist and not Buddhist.

Science
- Sit back-to-back. The partner facing the screen describes one of the minibeasts without mentioning its name. The other partner listens carefully and tries to accurately draw the minibeast (see Idea 85).
- Take it in turns to explain the digestive system, using as many of the target vocabulary words as you can. Your partner will give you points for every word you use correctly.

> **Teaching tip**
>
> Use talking points (see Idea 53) across the curriculum to discuss statements. Here are some examples.
>
> **Art and design:** Picasso *Weeping Woman* painting. 'Her face tells a story.', 'The bright colours are very cheerful.', 'It's hard to feel sorry for someone you don't actually know.'
>
> **DT:** 'Cooking is fun.', 'Cooking is one of the most important life skills.', 'Cooking is difficult.', 'We should try to eat seasonally.'
>
> **RE:** 'The rich should do more to help the poor.'

> **Bonus idea** ★
>
> Look up Concept Cartoons. They are often used in science but are useful across the curriculum, and it's easy to make up your own using children's misconceptions. Search for 'concept cartoon blank' for a template you can use.

IDEA 87

Oracy Skills Framework

The Oracy Skills Framework is a great planning tool. It has supported me in creating a yearly overview for our oracy lessons. *Deputy head*

The Oracy Skills Framework was created by Oracy Cambridge and Voice 21. It's a comprehensive breakdown of oracy skills.

Teaching tip

Search online for 'Oracy Skills Framework' to find a printable, colour version of the framework, plus some accompanying notes with detail about the key terms.

You could spend half a term focusing on each strand of the framework.

Taking it further

Show older pupils the framework. Give them copies to stick in their oracy jotters. Get them to reflect: 'Which oracy skills do you feel you have developed this term?', 'How are you progressing with voice projection?', 'Which part of the Oracy Skills Framework do you most need to work on?' Directly engaging with the framework like this will empower pupils to develop their own oracy skills.

Physical skills
- Voice – pace of speaking, tonal variation, clarity of pronunciation, voice projection.
- Body language – gesture and posture, facial expression and eye contact.

Cognitive skills
- Content – choice of content to convey meaning and intention, building on the views of others.
- Structure – structure and organisation of talk.
- Clarifying and summarising – seeking information and clarification through questions, summarising.
- Self-regulation – maintaining focus on task, time management.
- Reasoning – giving reasons to support views, critically examining ideas and views expressed.

Linguistic skills
- Vocabulary – appropriate vocabulary choice.
- Language – register, grammar.
- Rhetorical techniques – such as metaphor, humour, irony and mimicry.

Social and emotional skills
- Working with others – guiding or managing interactions, turn-taking.
- Listening and responding – listening actively and responding appropriately.
- Confidence in speaking – self-assurance, liveliness and flair.
- Audience awareness – taking account of level of understanding of the audience.

IDEA 88

Practising the four strands

The physical oracy strand has been brilliant with our EAL learners!
Oracy lead

Practical activities to develop skills across the four strands of the Oracy Skills Framework.

Physical
- Play Tikidoo! Display a made-up word, such as 'tikidoo', and ask pupils to try saying it with different emotions: happy, sad, angry, calm, excited and so on. A great game to play with tone of voice, facial expressions and gestures.
- See also Ideas 28, 29, 38, 62, 76 and 83.

Linguistic
- Play Persuade me! Give pupils a fun scenario such as 'Persuade your partner to take up unicycling!' Each pupil has 30 seconds to persuade their partner, and they must use at least one of these three linguistic techniques: rhetorical question, repetition, humour. At the end of the 30 seconds, the partner gives feedback about which techniques they noticed.
- See also Ideas 33, 69, 78, 79 and 95.

Cognitive
- Discuss thought experiments and moral dilemmas with your class: 'You find some money on a busy street – what do you do?', 'What would you do if you could turn invisible?'
- See also Ideas 57, 72, 73, 78 and 81.

Social and emotional
- Play Grab the audience: In trios, pupils take turns to tell the start of a story (for example, about a dog who saved someone's life). Their challenge is to speak as if to different audiences, for example children, elderly people, parents or a VIP. What will they say or change to engage each audience? How will they speak?
- See also Ideas 6, 23, 24, 37, 43, 46 and 81.

> **Teaching tip**
>
> Search online for 'thunks' – great challenges to further develop the cognitive strand.

> **Bonus idea** ★
>
> Get pupils to try some tongue twisters. These are fun and a good way to work on clarity of pronunciation (physical strand).

IDEA 89

Vision for talk

The children are more articulate now, without a shadow of doubt.
Executive head, reflecting on the oracy journey of her three schools

Here are some vision statements for oracy. Use this as a checklist or as a guide for action planning.

Teaching tip

Reflect on and act on your vision statements one at a time. For example, focus on one per term. The ideas in this book will help you achieve your vision.

Taking it further

Search online for 'Voice 21 benchmarks' to find an inspiring and detailed framework for implementing oracy in schools. See also case studies in Rupert Knight's excellent book *Classroom Talk* (2020).

Pupils
Pupils actively listen to their peers.
Pupils express themselves audibly and clearly, using appropriate powerful and specific language.
Pupils give detail, explanations and reasons without being prompted.
Pupils are confident to share partial thinking.
Pupils respond thoughtfully, building on or challenging each other's points.
Pupils ask relevant questions (to each other and to the adults).
All pupils participate in talk in all formats (whole-class/pair/group).
Learning talk is productive and has impact in all formats.
Pupils understand that different situations require different kinds of talk and listening.
Pupils enjoy classroom talk and know that it helps them learn.

Teachers (including learning support staff)
Teacher talk is respectful, concise and effective.
Teachers model high-quality talk, thinking and listening.
Questioning is effective, for example planned questions and probing questions.
Pupils have 'thinking time' after questions.
Learning through dialogue is a key approach.
Challenging discussion questions are a core part of curriculum and pedagogy.
Teachers enjoy oracy, and value its positive impact on learning and relationships.

IDEA 90

Talk promise

The talk promise helps boost my confidence because I know a lot more people will be listening. *Age 10*

A whole-school agreement for talking and listening.

Having a whole-school agreement, promise, or pledge for talking and listening immediately raises the status of oracy with staff, pupils and parents. Here is an example from a school:

Our talk pledge
- We show we are listening by looking at the speaker.
- We join in because all ideas lead to learning.
- We speak in a clear voice that can be heard by everyone.
- We give each other time to think.
- We build on, or challenge with respect, each other's ideas.
- We ask questions if we don't understand or would like to learn more.

Some schools decide to start their talk agreement with a statement about the value of talk, e.g., 'We use talk to help us learn.'

Schools that work on their pledge or promise collaboratively with staff and pupils have more 'buy in' than leaders simply imposing a set of rules. Here are some ideas to make it a participatory process:

- Give out some sample 'rules' and ask people to decide in small groups which three are the most important.
- Ranking activity — order possible elements from least important to most important.
- Teachers come up with a draft agreement and the School Council make comments and suggestions.

Teaching tip
Make sure every class has copies of your talk agreement and that it is displayed in letters big enough for everyone to read no matter where they are sitting.

Taking it further
Put your talk agreement on your website, or make it into postcards to send home to parents.

Bonus idea ★
Have a whole-school assembly to launch your talk agreement. Get children to lead. Celebrate how valuable learning talk can be. (This is particularly important when children are used to being told 'stop talking!')

IDEA 91

Talking Tuesdays

Talking Tuesdays really helped me grow my confidence because I was anxious about speaking in front of my class but now, with lots of practice, I am not! *Age 8*

Put oracy on your timetable! Allow time each week to practise and develop oracy skills with your pupils.

If you want your pupils to become better at talking — so that they gain a life skill and are able to use talk for learning — they need to have time to practise. Having a weekly talk lesson is a great way to do this.

A weekly slot is also an opportunity for you as a teacher to try things out — to become more confident and skilled with talk techniques.

Putting oracy on your timetable sends a strong message to everyone that talk is important, and that we need to learn how to do it well.

Decide how much time to dedicate. You could allocate anything from five minutes upwards; even a short lesson each week will reap rewards.

Some schools call this 'Talking Tuesdays'. For example, 9:00–9.30 am every Tuesday morning, the whole school is focusing on oracy. Everybody's talking!

Ideas for oracy lessons
- Plan lessons in relation to the Oracy Skills Framework (Idea 87), focusing on different skills throughout the year.
- Focus on different talk formats, such as pair talk, whole-class talk, exploratory talk in small groups and presentational talk. Spend half a term practising and developing each one.
- Play talk games (see Part 8).
- Collect pupil voice around talk (see Idea 99).
- See also Idea 93.

> **Taking it further**
>
> As part of your weekly talk lesson, allow a few minutes for individual pupils to present on a topic they are interested in. One-minute speeches work well, especially when combined with peer feedback (see Idea 8). Create a rota of all your pupils. Ask them to prepare and practise their speeches at home, remembering to focus on the oracy skills they've been learning.

IDEA 92

Let's talk about talk

Talking is useful... You must control what you say, though, or things can go wrong! *Age 7*

Pupils need to know the importance of oracy to fully engage with developing the skills. Dedicate time to talk about talk.

Here are some prompts and questions:

Talk prompt starters about talk
Outside school, I use talk to...
Talking has helped me to...
I once used a loud voice to...
I once had to speak very politely when...

Talking points – do you agree or disagree with these statements? (See Idea 53)
Talking and thinking are the same thing.
Two heads are usually better than one for solving problems.
We must be quiet to learn.
We learn by reading and writing, not by talking.

Questions about talk
Would you rather talk to a pet or a toy?
Would you rather talk all day or listen all day?
Would you rather make a speech or have a discussion?
How can we make sure everyone's voice is heard?
Are you better at talking or listening?
How do people learn to talk?
Who do you like talking to? Why?
When are you asked not to talk? Why?
When is it difficult to talk to other people?
How would you communicate with other people if you couldn't talk?
How many different languages can you speak?
What happens when people talk but others don't listen?
Is it helpful to have silent time?

Teaching tip

Vary the discussion format from pairs to groups to whole-class, so that while your pupils are talking about talk they have opportunities to develop different oracy skills.

IDEA 93

Oracy lesson structure

We practise lots of ways of talking and how to be good listeners. I have joined the school production and have a speaking part, which I would not have done before this year! Age 9

A simple four-part structure to help plan 30-minute oracy lessons.

Teaching tip

Use your oracy lessons to practise some of the structures and techniques from this book. Your pupils will then be ready to use them across the curriculum. For example, if you want to recap prior learning in history, use Find someone who... (Idea 70). Practise it first in your oracy lesson using fun or talk-focused questions.

Part 1: Let's warm up our voices (5 mins)
This stage of the lesson is about getting everyone talking – for example in pairs or in unison. You could play a talk game (see Part 8) or do some fun voice activities (search online for 'Drama Toolkit voice' for some helpful ideas).

Part 2: Let's talk about talk (5 mins)
See Idea 92.

Part 3: Let's work on our oracy skills (15 mins)
This is the most important part of the lesson. Choose a skill that you want your class to get better at. Use the Oracy Skills Framework to help you (Idea 87). Plan carefully, and be as rigorous around skill development as you would be in any other lesson.

Part 4: Let's reflect (5 mins)
As with any part of the curriculum, pupils need time to think about what they are getting better at and what they are finding tricky. Here are some prompts for verbal reflections:
- An oracy skill that our class is getting better at is...
- An oracy skill that I would like to get better at is...
- A person who impressed me with their oracy skills today was...
- Using gestures when we speak can...
- Today, my attempts at summarising were...

IDEA 94

Are they getting better at talking?

We get to tell each other what we're learning. *Age 7*

Tips for monitoring and assessing oracy.

Here are some questions for pupils to reflect on. Compare their responses throughout the year.
- What helps you when you need to talk to your whole class?
- What makes it more difficult?
- Are you becoming a more confident talker?
- Are you becoming a better listener?
- Who is a great speaker in your class? What do they do that impresses you?
- Who is a good listener? How do you know?
- What do you do if you disagree?

Pupils complete a reflection, for example at the end of every oracy lesson or at the end of every day or week. Provide them with self-assessment grids using statements such as these, from *Talk Box* by Lyn Dawes and Claire Sams:
☐ I talked to the whole class.
☐ I asked a question.
☐ I answered a question.
☐ I gave a reason.
☐ I said what I thought.
☐ I listened carefully.
☐ I joined in.
☐ I liked talking to my group.
☐ I found it hard to talk.
☐ I found it hard to listen.
☐ We could not agree.
☐ We decided together.

Remember – the best evidence comes from talking to the children. Invite colleagues into your class to see how much oracy has improved!

Teaching tip

Use specific praise about talk often, so that children realise what they are doing well.

This will also help you realise what your class are doing well. You can then decide to use particular praise phrases to highlight oracy skills that you want other children to develop: 'I loved the way you asked Jason to clarify.'

Taking it further

Check out the dialogic teaching questionnaire in the online T-SEDA toolkit.

Bonus idea ★

Peer assessment is also a valuable tool. Search online for 'Voice 21 Talk Detectives'.

IDEA 95

Use talk to develop vocabulary

A playful approach to word activities is low risk and enables conversations to go beyond the boundaries of definitions to explore deeper meanings and understanding. *Jane Yates, P4C trainer*

Plan talk tasks that allow pupils to use target words.

Teaching tip

Have high expectations; insist that pupils use target words when they are speaking in lessons:

Teacher: What is happening with these magnets?
Pupil: They're pushing each other!
Teacher: Yes, now say it again using our focus vocabulary.
Pupil: They're repelling each other!

Taking it further

Check out *Bringing Words to Life* (Beck, McKeown and Kucan, 2013). Also look at the excellent 'Summary Bullseye' activity in *Transform Teaching and Learning through Talk* (Gaunt and Stott, 2019).

Here are some of the key messages from the research on vocabulary development:
- **Teach it** – don't just expect children to absorb new words.
- Provide opportunities to **play with words**.
- Arrange **frequent encounters** with new words (at least six exposures).
- Encourage active **thinking about words and meanings** in a range of contexts.

Oral rehearsal: This sounds obvious, but don't forget to do it! Pupils need time to say the new word aloud – lots of times. For example, 'So, insects that move pollen from plant to plant are called pollinators. Let's all say that together... pollinators! One more time... pollinators! Your turn Naomi. [Naomi says 'Pollinators!'] Yes – good pronunciation. Everyone again, pollinators! Read out the definition, Luke. [Pollinators are...] Thank you. So, how would you explain in your own words what a pollinator is? [Pause for thinking time, then cold call.] Leila? [A pollinator is...] Now, everyone with your talk partner think of at least three pollinators. Then I'll use the lolly sticks.'

Talk structures: Spend ten minutes every day exploring and playing with words through simple talk tasks. Use familiar, straightforward structures again and again to make planning easy. For example, Would you rather, Good idea/bad idea?, Odd one out (Ideas 71, 72 and 73).

Imagine you decide to teach the 'tier 2' words 'assume' and 'compare'. Start as normal by looking at meaning, spelling and examples in sentences. Then provide opportunities for further thinking and talking about these words. Ask things like:

- Would you rather someone assumed something about you or compared you to someone else?
- What is the opposite of 'assume'?
- Comparing your house to someone else's: good idea/bad idea?

Here's another example for younger children. You want to teach the verbs 'create' and 'estimate'.

- Would you rather create something from wooden blocks or from paper?
- Would you rather estimate the number of marbles in a jar or children in a playground?
- What is the opposite of 'create'?
- Estimate instead of count: good idea/bad idea?

Or, you're reading *Skellig* by David Almond and you realise that your pupils don't understand certain words that you assumed they'd know. After explaining meanings and showing images, use structures to address this vocabulary gap. For example: 'Which is the odd one out: chest of drawers, deckchair, wash basin? Why?' Pupils will start to think and say things such as 'Well, maybe the wash basin is different because the other two are made from wood.' Or, 'I think that the deckchair is the odd one out because it's not usually found inside a house.'

These techniques are deceptively simple. Yet they give pupils both the frequent encounters they need with new words, as well as opportunities to think about and understand them more deeply.

Teaching tip

Take the decision to deliberately teach between five and ten words every week. Plan frequent encounters — at least six separate encounters with each of the chosen words, spread throughout the week.

Bonus idea ★

Set up activities around concepts from across the curriculum. For example, create collections of synonyms and antonyms of the concept. Ask pupils to sort them into two groups — related to the concept and not related to the concept. Or ask them to rank them from same meaning to different meaning.

Alternatively, create examples and non-examples of the concept, and ask pupils to sort them. Make some deliberately challenging, to generate engaging and meaningful dialogue.

IDEA 96

Talk-based outcomes

We used to rely entirely on written outcomes to see how much our pupils had learned. Now we're starting to use talk-based outcomes.
Deputy head

Outcomes are planned moments, after a period of learning, where children have an opportunity to apply, showcase and celebrate their new vocabulary, skills and knowledge. There are many ways to do this using talk.

Teaching tip

When you observe talk-based outcomes, make sure you're clear about what you're watching and listening for – subject content and oracy skills are two separate things.

Taking it further

Get organised! Have recording devices available and charged so you can easily capture your class talking about what they've learned.

Bonus idea ★

Organise termly talk-based outcome showcase celebration events.

- **DT:** Informative speeches to parents about healthy eating and seasonality.
- **English:** Persuasive audio message for the school website about parking outside school.
- **Art:** Class debate, 'graffiti is wrong', after learning about street art.
- **Science:** Presentations to the class in pairs about the amazing powers of magnets. (Consider speaking frames – see Idea 33.)
- **Science:** Record a voiceover for images or diagrams on slides explaining the water cycle.
- **History:** Groups perform two-minute plays about life in the Stone Age, each covering at least three different aspects.
- **Geography:** Group discussions about the talking point 'All trade should be fair trade'.

For live discussions and presentations, consider inviting visitors. Pupils from other year groups, staff and parents are easily accessible audiences. Also consider audio or video recording.

Be sure to teach the specific oracy skills relevant to each chosen outcome. So, if you want your class to do a presentation about the Tudors, give them opportunities to learn and practise the oracy skills of presenting to an audience.

(Remember that debates, discussions and role play can still also be used to help children explore and learn *throughout* a topic.)

IDEA 97

Oracy opportunities

Oracy has made me funnier! *Oracy Club participant, age 9*

Weave oracy into every aspect of school life.

On behalf of the class: On school trips or when you have visitors in your classroom, invite a few pupils to show their appreciation. 'Juanito, please could you say something to our visitor on behalf of the class.'

Voicemail: Have pupils record the answerphone message for your school. When parents or other callers phone, they will immediately know that this is a school where children's voices are valued.

Greeting visitors: Whenever you have visitors to your school, organise opportunities for pupils to greet them and explain key information or achievements.

Extracurricular events: Poetry Cafe, speech competitions, storytelling evenings.

Extracurricular clubs: Oracy Club, Philosophy Club, Debating Club, Public Speaking Club, Spoken Word Club.

School welcome video: Make videos for your school website, with pupils giving welcome messages and key information: uniform, parking, walking to school, healthy dinners, upcoming events, etc.

School events: Arrange for pupils to open and close all school events with short speeches, from assemblies to sports day to winter fair to graduation.

Parents' evening: Have pupils greet parents, ask them to fill in the parent survey, and so on.

> **Teaching tip**
>
> Give all your pupils access to additional oracy opportunities. If you only give opportunities to your 'best speakers', then only they will improve!

> **Taking it further**
>
> Run oracy skills workshops with groups of pupils to enable them to take on special roles such as playground buddies and peer mediators.

> **Bonus idea** ★
>
> Oracy ambassadors: Each half-term, give five pupils in your class the role of oracy ambassador. They can deliver messages, speak for the class in assemblies, ask questions at the office, befriend children in the playground, and more! This is a chance to really push themselves to develop and practise their oracy skills.

IDEA 98

Parental engagement

Great talk prompts for parents! *SENDCo*
Exactly what our parents need. *Headteacher*

Ways to get families talking more with their children, including some handy prompts.

Teaching tip

Search online for 'Topsy Page parent talk moves' to find a printable resource.

Taking it further

Get hold of the brilliant and accessible book *How to Talk so Kids Will Listen and Listen so Kids Will Talk* (Faber and Mazlish, 2012).

Key message for parents

Talking develops confidence, ideas, reasoning and ability to work with others. It can also contribute to improved reading, writing and maths.

Tips for parents

- Make sure you genuinely listen to your child's thoughts and ideas. Don't guess what they're going to say or finish their sentences!
- Set aside some daily time for talking, for example teatime.
- Don't push if they aren't in the mood for talking. Wait for something that sparks their interest. Then listen.
- Don't bombard them with questions. Ask fewer questions and give them space to talk.

Talk moves for parents

To get children interested in talking: Ask thought-provoking or funny questions. For example: 'Would you rather eat spiders or ants?', 'Should people have to pay for food?'

Tell them what you are impressed by: 'You're so good at thinking!', 'Great listening, Ali.', 'Thanks for disagreeing calmly, Sam.' (Instead of 'well done', 'good girl', etc.)

Show interest: 'Go on…', 'That's interesting…', 'Tell me more.', 'I'd love to hear your idea.'

Encourage critical thinking: 'How do you know?', 'Convince me!', 'Is that always true?'

IDEA 99

What do your pupils think about oracy?

I like it because we get to talk to each other. Age 5

It takes courage to ask for honest feedback, but ultimately, listening to pupils will help you to plan and teach better.

Here are some examples of pupil voice questions you could use. Pick questions relevant to where you are on your oracy journey.

- What do you think of how we use talk in our lessons? Does the talking help you learn?
- What do you think of oracy lessons? What do you like? What do you find challenging?
- What do you think of our talk prompts?
- What do you think of talk partners?
- When you talk in groups, how does it go?
- What do you think of standing up to talk to the class sometimes?
- What do you think of lolly sticks? (See Idea 20.)
- What do you think of our talk promise/ground rules? (See Ideas 90 and 49.)
- What do you think of the Oracy Skills Framework? Does it help you?
- What could help you become a better talker?
- What could help everyone join in?

You can collect pupil voice in different ways, for example talking to children in small groups and noting down their thoughts. Or, in whole-class, ask pupils to make individual notes, and optionally follow this with class dialogue. Whichever approach you choose, keep a record of pupil comments and take time to reflect on your next steps. Each time you get feedback from pupils, try to make at least one tweak to your practice.

For more pupil voice questions, see Idea 100.

Teaching tip

Reflect critically on what pupils tell you – are they making valid points? Do you agree with their suggestions? If they say things you don't agree with, try to figure out where they're coming from – there might be something worth exploring.

IDEA 100

Leading oracy

The biggest thing is modelling and integrity. Your team need to know you believe in it. Lead by example at all times. Show that you're putting in the leg work as well. *Deputy head*

Top tips to develop and embed oracy across your school.

Teaching tip

Include lunchtime staff, office staff and teaching assistants. For example, agree that all staff will aim to have at least one high-quality two-minute conversation with a child every day outside lessons.

Taking it further

In collaboration with senior leaders, make a policy decision to use talk-based outcomes (Idea 96) as part of capturing and celebrating learning. To facilitate this, organise permissions, processes and tech for audio and video recording. (Use some of this footage to put children's voices at the heart of your school website.)

As with leading any subject, you'll want to make an action plan, create systems, organise professional development, find ways to check progress, look to the long term and continually keep everyone consistently focused on the vision (Idea 89). Here are some specific pointers for leading oracy.

Be the change
Whatever oracy strategies you ask your team to use, make sure you're using them as well. You can even use the strategies in staff meetings to get colleagues familiar with them and put everyone in the children's shoes. For example, in your assemblies and staff meetings:
- Use talk prompts on slides (Idea 18).
- Cold call, after thinking time: 'Tash, what do you think about this?' (Idea 21).
- Change the seating to a circle (Idea 59).
- Use partner talk techniques (see Part 4).

Have a set of lolly sticks ready for staff meetings to hear different people's thoughts at key moments. For assemblies, ask each class to bring their labelled pot of sticks, to enable you to randomly select children from different classes to speak. (See Idea 20.)

Collect pupil voice to inspire, challenge and motivate your colleagues
Children's words can be compelling and convincing. Find out what they think about oracy, and take time to reflect with colleagues (see Idea 99).

Here are some further pupil voice questions that will help you gain insight into classroom practice across your school:
- How is the balance of learning talk in your lessons – do adults talk more or do children talk more?
- Do children listen well to each other in lessons? How do you know?
- How often do you do 'talk partners'? How often do you change partners?
- When your teachers ask the class a question, how do they decide who answers?
- Do you have ground rules for group talk?
- If you want to challenge something another pupil has said, how do you do that?
- Do you have opportunities to talk about things that are going on in the world?

Create a bank of inspiring quotes from your pupils, to display and show in staff meetings throughout the year.

Build dialogue among staff
One of the most effective ways to improve and develop practice is through collaborative dialogue. Encourage and enable your teacher colleagues to have dialogue about oracy:
- Discuss oracy strategies: What's working? What isn't? Why? Is the pace of change manageable? Which pupils are responding well? What can be done to support others?
- Watch each other teach and discuss afterwards the impact of different oracy strategies on different children.
- Problem-solve and share good practice together – one teacher might be wondering how to empower a child to speak in their class, or seeking ideas for a purposeful talk task for a particular curriculum area.
- Be proactive in creating time for dialogue: help organise cover and request slots in staff meetings, phase meetings and CPD days.
- Organise whole-school focus moments: 'This week let's all try hand signals in class discussions – we'll review the impact at next week's staff meeting.'

> **Teaching tip**
>
> Consider organising 'lesson study' to develop oracy in your school. This is an effective and enjoyable way to improve practice involving joint planning, focusing on specific pupils, watching lessons and collaborative dialogue with colleagues. Search online for 'lesson study handbook' to get started.

> **Bonus idea** ★
>
> Encourage teachers to incorporate oracy objectives into lessons. 'Remember, our oracy objective for this lesson is to use a loud voice so everyone can hear our ideas.' Or, 'Remember, our oracy objective this week is giving reasons and evidence for our thinking.'

References and further reading

Alexander, R. (2020) *A Dialogic Teaching Companion.* Abingdon, Oxon: Routledge

Barnes, D. (2008) 'Exploratory talk for learning', in N. Mercer and S. Hodgkinson (eds), Exploring *Talk in School.* London: Sage

Beck, I.L., McKeown, M.G. and Kucan, L. (2013) *Bringing Words to Life: Robust Vocabulary Instruction.* New York: Guilford Press

Burningham, J. (1978) *Would You Rather.* London: Jonathan Cape

Cain, S. (2016) *Quiet Power.* London: Penguin

Chapin, S., O'Connor, C. and Anderson, N.C. (2022) *Talk Moves: A Teacher's Guide for Using Classroom Discussions in Math, Grades K-6* (3rd edn.). London: Heinemann

Dawes, L. (2011) *Creating a Speaking and Listening Classroom: Integrating Talk for Learning at Key Stage 2.* Abingdon, Oxon: Routledge

Dawes, L. (2012) *Talking Points: Discussion Activities in the Primary Classroom.* Abingdon, Oxon: Routledge

Dawes, L. and Sams, C. (2004) *Talk Box – Speaking and Listening Activities for Learning at Key Stage 1.* London: David Fulton

de Bono, E. (2023), 'For schools and families', www.debono.com/schools-and-families.

Dweck, C.S. (2007) 'The perils and promises of praise', *Educational Leadership*, 65, (2), 34–39

Faber, A. and Mazlish, E. (2001) *How to Talk so Kids Will Listen and Listen so Kids Will Talk.* London: Piccadilly Press (first published 1982, Avon Books)

Gaunt, A. and Stott, A. (2019) *Transform Teaching and Learning Through Talk: The Oracy Imperative.* London: Rowan & Littlefield

Howe, A. and Johnson, J. (1992) *Common Bonds: Storytelling in the Classroom.* London: Hodder & Stoughton

Johnson, M. and Wintgens, A. (2012) *Can I Tell You About Selective Mutism? A Guide for Friends, Family and Professionals.* London: Jessica Kingsley Publishers

Knight, R. (2020) *Classroom Talk: Evidence-Based Teaching for Enquiring Teachers.* St Albans: Critical Publishing

Lee, W. (2018), 'How inclusive is oracy?' Oracy Cambridge blog, oracycambridge.org/how-inclusive-is-oracy

Lemov, D. et al. (2023), 'Teach Like a Champion', teachlikeachampion.org

Mannion, J. and McAllister, K. (2020) *Fear is the Mind Killer.* Woodbridge, Suffolk: John Catt Educational

Mercer, N. (2019) *Language and the Joint Creation of Knowledge.* Abingdon, Oxon: Routledge

Mercer, N. and Hodgkinson, S. (eds) (2008) *Exploring Talk in Schools.* London: Sage Publications

Oracy Cambridge and Voice 21 (2019) 'Oracy Skills Framework', oracycambridge.org/wp-content/uploads/2020/06/The-Oracy-Skills-Framework-and-Glossary.pdf

Phillipson, N. (2023) 'Teachers' guide to dialogic pedagogy', http://21stcenturylearners.org.uk/?p=1337

Resnick, L. B., Asterhan, C.S.C. and Clarke, S. N. (2018) 'Accountable talk: instructional dialogue that builds the mind', UNESCO International Bureau of Education, https://unesdoc.unesco.org/ark:/48223/pf0000262675

Rothstein, D. and Santana, L. (2011) *Make Just One Change.* Cambridge, Massachusetts/MA: Harvard Education Press

Rowe, M.B. (1986) 'Wait time: slowing down may be a way of speeding up!', *Journal of Teacher Education*, 37, 43–50

Stahl (1994) 'Using "think-time" and "wait-time" skillfully in the classroom', ERIC Digest. https://files.eric.ed.gov/fulltext/ED370885.pdf

Stanley, S. (2012) *Why Think? Philosophical Play from 3–11.* London: Continuum

Stanley, S. with Bowkett, S. (2004) *But Why? Developing Philosophical Thinking in the Classroom.* Stafford: Network Educational Press

Sutcliffe, R., Bigglestone, T. and Buckley, J. (2019) *Thinking Moves A to Z: Metacognition Made Simple.* London: Dialogue Works

Thom, J. (2020) *A Quiet Education: Challenging the Extrovert Ideal in our Schools.* Woodbridge, Suffolk: John Catt Educational

Tough, J. (1979) *Talk for Learning and Teaching.* London: Schools Council Publications Ward Lock Educational